INTERACTIVE CITATION WORKBOOK FOR
ALWD CITATION MANUAL
2009 Edition

INTERACTIVE CITATION WORKBOOK FOR *ALWD CITATION MANUAL*

2009 Edition

Tracy L. McGaugh
Associate Professor of Legal Process
Touro Law Center

Christine Hurt
Professor of Law
University of Illinois College of Law

 LexisNexis

ISBN: 978-1-4224-2958-7

Editorial Offices
121 Chanlon Rd., New Providence, NJ 07974 (908) 464-6800
201 Mission St., San Francisco, CA 94105-1831 (415) 908-3200
www.lexisnexis.com

MATTHEW◆BENDER

TABLE OF CONTENTS

TABLE OF CONTENTS

ACKNOWLEDGMENTS

It takes a village to create the ICW! The ICW is made possible by the tremendous support we receive from our families, friends, research assistants, secretaries and law schools. Specifically, we would like to thank the Marquette University Law School, South Texas College of Law, and University of Illinois College of Law, and of course, our first—year law students. We are especially indebted to Sean Caldwell at LexisNexis for ushering us into the next phase of the ICW. This year, we extend a special thanks to Robin Meyer of the University of Texas for providing us with advance notice of the *Texas Rules of Form* changes so we could update Chapter 11 for the 11th edition of *Texas Rules of Form.*

USING THE INTERACTIVE CITATION WORKBOOK

Layout of the Workbook

The ICW contains eighteen citation exercises. Each exercise builds on and reinforces the skills learned in previous exercises. The goal of this learning method is for you to become familiar with the organization and use of the *ALWD* (pronounced "Allwood") *Citation Manual.**

You need not memorize the citation rules. However, through repeated use, you will probably find that you have memorized the commonly-used rules.

Each ICW chapter consists of explanatory text and a citation exercise. The text will introduce and explain the rules needed for that exercise, demonstrate by example how those rules are used, and give a checklist you can use in drafting your citations for that exercise. Because each exercise builds on previous exercises, you might find each checklist helpful for many of the later exercises as well. The exercises may be completed in the Workbook and turned in, or you may transfer your answers to the Workstation for immediate feedback. Check with your instructor to see which method you should use.

Beginning to Use the *ALWD Manual*

The *ALWD Manual* is divided into several major sections. To help you navigate it more easily, you may want to tab the sections of the *ALWD Manual* you will use most: Citation Basics, Cases, Statutes, Appendix 1, Appendix 2, Appendix 3, Appendix 4, and the Index. Before you begin any ICW exercises, you should read the Introductory Material section. Pay particular attention to the section titled "How to Use This Book." Although the index gets only a one-sentence mention in the subsection called "Finding Tools," the index can be tremendously helpful to you. If you have a question about drafting a citation, and you have no idea where to start, the index is your best bet.

The *ALWD Manual* is currently in its Third Edition. If changes or updates need to be made before the Fourth Edition is published, they will be posted at http://www.alwd.org.

Getting Started on the Exercises

The Interactive Citation Workbook and Workstation (both "ICW") will help you learn the citation rules you will use most frequently when you clerk for a law firm or a court and, later, practice law. The ICW does not cover the rules that most practitioners rarely, if ever, use. However, after completing the ICW exercises, you should be comfortable enough with the *ALWD Manual* as a reference guide that you can find rules you need to cite any authority.

Legal citation has specific requirements for typeface. Those requirements are found in Rule 1.0. Although Rule 1.0 allows for italics as either *slanted type* or <u>underlining</u>, the ICW provides for only *slanted type*. Punctuation in combination with italicized

---

* Excerpts from the *ALWD Manual* used with permission of the copyright holders: The Association of Legal Writing Directors, Darby Dickerson, and Aspen Law and Business.

material should be italicized according to Rule 1.4. In addition to typeface requirements, citation has specific spacing requirements. Those requirements are found in Rule 2.2.

Using the Interactive Citation Workstation

You may complete your exercises online. Your professor should tell you whether this is a requirement or not. The Interactive Citation Workstation (ICW) will give you immediate feedback on the citations you draft for these exercises. Probably, the bulk of the time you spend on the ICW exercises will be in drafting your first attempt at the citation. Therefore, if you share a computer with someone or are billed for Internet access on the basis of the amount of time spent online, you may want to do the initial work on paper to minimize your time online.

When you finish the results online, you can email those results to your professor from the ICW, or you can print out the results. If you e-mail the results, it is still a good idea to print and keep a copy of the results as confirmation that you completed an exercise and to use as a personal reference or study guide.

The ICW is located at http://lexisnexis.com/icw/. The complete instructions for using the Workstation are on the web site. To save time in completing the exercises, you should read these online instructions before beginning the first exercise online.

Chapter 1

CASE NAMES

Legal citation, like citation in other disciplines, identifies the source of an idea that a writer uses in his or her writing. A legal citation to a judicial opinion (a "case") has three basic components, all of which are given in the heading of every judicial opinion: the case name, the volume and page number of the source the opinion is printed in (the "reporter"), and a parenthetical that includes the identification of the court that issued the opinion and the date of the opinion. The first three exercises of the ICW will acquaint you with how to use the information given in the heading of an opinion to draft a basic legal citation. As you read the text in each ICW chapter, you may find it helpful to refer to the *ALWD* rules mentioned so you can familiarize yourself with both the content and location of the rules. Also, the examples provided in the *ALWD Manual* following each rule will be helpful in understanding the rule itself.

The "formula" for a basic legal citation follows:

Party 1 v. Party 2, Vol. Reporter Pg. (Court Date).

A. Using Typeface

The first part of a citation is the case name (*Party 1 v. Party 2*). The case name is made up of the names of the parties. Looking at the citation formula above, you will notice that the case name (*Party 1 v. Party 2*) is italicized. This follows *ALWD* Rules 1.1 and 1.3, which allow for either *italicizing* or underlining the entire case name. When you type your citations in the ICW, you will use italics. Otherwise, you should check with your instructor or supervising attorney for his or her preference. What you might not notice at first glance is that the comma following the case name is *not* italicized. This follows Rule 1.4, which tells you not to italicize punctuation when it *follows* italicized material. Italicize punctuation only if it is *within* the italicized material.

B. Shortening Party Information

The party information is given at the beginning of a court opinion in the heading. You should list parties in the order they are given in the heading, regardless of procedural posture (*e.g.*, if the defendant is listed first in the heading, list him or her first in the citation). Because cases may involve multiple parties, one or more of which may have a lengthy name, the *ALWD Manual* provides a system of rules for shortening the case name so that the citation to an opinion is not cumbersome, yet still sufficiently identifies the primary parties. These rules are found in 12.2 with some additional guidance on abbreviations coming from Appendix 3 in the back of the *ALWD Manual*.

The rules in 12.2 fall into two general categories: rules calling for omissions and rules calling for abbreviations. Read these rules carefully before attempting the Case Names exercise.

You **should omit** the following general types of information from the citation:

- any actions other than the first in a consolidated case (12.2(b)(1))
- any parties other than the first listed on each side (12.2(c)(1))
- phrases indicating multiple parties (12.2(c)(2))
- descriptive terms (12.2(c)(3)) or official titles (12.2(k)) for parties identified by name
- abbreviations such as "d/b/a" following business names (12.2(e)(1))
- given names or initials of *individuals* (12.2(d)), but not in the name of a business (12.2(e)(2))
- "State of," "Commonwealth of," and "People of," unless the party name is the same as the state the opinion is from. In that case, use only "State," "Commonwealth," or "People" (12.2(h))[1]
- the name of the Commissioner of Internal Revenue (12.2(j))
- all but the first-listed piece of property when property is a party (12.2(m))
- "The" as the first word in a party name (12.2(q))

You **may omit** the following information from the citation:

- the second business designation when a name includes two or more business designations (12.2(e)(7))
- longer geographical references when a city or municipality is a party (12.2(i))

You **should abbreviate** words in a citation in the following circumstances:

- "versus" to "v." (12.2(c)(4))
- "United States" to "U.S." (12.2(g))
- "Commissioner of Internal Revenue" to "Commr." (12.2(j))
- relator information to "ex rel." (12.2(n))
- procedural phrases (12.2(o))

You **may abbreviate** the following words in a citation sentence:

- any word of an organization's name listed in Appendix 3 (12.2(e)(3))[2]
- a party name to widely-recognized initials (12.2(e)(6))

You **should not abbreviate** the following:

- any word not listed in Appendix 3 (12.2(e)(3))

When drafting a case name, first omit the necessary information and then abbreviate the rest. Let's try an example before you tackle the Case Names exercise.

---

[1] For governmental entities whose names are given as "The People of the State of" or "The Commonwealth of the State of," use "People" and "Commonwealth" respectively.

[2] Anytime the *ALWD Manual* gives you the option of abbreviating, the ICW will expect you to do so.

Southwest Engineering Company and John Doe, Defendants-Appellants, versus United States of America, Plaintiff-Appellee

First, let's **omit** all information that the rules require. Rule 12.2(c)(1) requires that we omit all parties other than the first; so we will omit "and John Doe" from the first party:

Southwest Engineering Company ~~and John Doe~~, Defendants-Appellants, versus United States of America, Plaintiff-Appellee

Rule 12.2(c)(3) requires that we omit descriptive terms for named parties, so we will delete "Defendants-Appellants" and "Plaintiff-Appellee":

Southwest Engineering Company ~~and John Doe, Defendants-Appellants~~, versus The United States of America, ~~Plaintiff-Appellee~~

Rule 12.2(g) requires that we cite "United States of America" as "U.S.":

Southwest Engineering Company ~~and John Doe, Defendants-Appellants~~, versus U.S., ~~Plaintiff-Appellee~~

Now that we have omitted all of the words *ALWD* requires, let's **abbreviate** what's left. First, we abbreviate "versus" to "v." following Rule 12.2(c)(4).

Southwest Engineering Company ~~and John Doe, Defendants-Appellants~~, v. U.S., ~~Plaintiff-Appellee~~

Then, we look in Appendix 3 to see which words in "Southwest Engineering Company" should be abbreviated. We notice that all three words are listed in Appendix 3; so we abbreviate those words:

S.W. Engr. Co. ~~and John Doe, Defendants-Appellants~~, v. U.S., ~~Plaintiff-Appellee~~

Now, all we have to do is italicize the case name, and it's ready to take its place in a citation sentence!

S.W. Engr. Co. v. U.S.

Checklist for Case Names

- Have you italicized the case name?
- Have you omitted words according to 12.2?

    - additional parties or actions
    - given names or initials of individuals
    - geographical terms and locations as necessary
    - surplus business designation names
    - surplus pieces of property

- Have you abbreviated words according to 12.2?

    - "versus" to "v."
    - "United States" to "U.S."
    - "Commissioner of Internal Revenue" to "Commr."
    - relator information to "ex rel."
    - procedural phrases
    - words listed in Appendix 3
    - an organization name to widely-recognized initials

Exercise 1

Case Names

Put the following case name information in correct *ALWD* citation form. All cases are being cited in citation sentences unless the problem indicates otherwise. This exercise focuses on Rule 12.

If *ALWD* allows for an abbreviation or omission, the correct answer on the ICW will incorporate that abbreviation or omission.

Before beginning the online exercises, complete the online intro quiz.

1. A single action styled Frank Messina v. William W. Burden, Leonard Armstrong v. Dennis R. Johnson

   _____

   _____

2. C.A. Nelson, appellee, versus City of Las Vegas, appellant

   _____

   _____

3. The Estate of Mary Sanders

   _____

   _____

4. Eleanor and Kenneth Van Buskirk, petitioners, versus Carey Canadian Mines, Limited, respondent

   _____

   _____

5. Sabine Pilot Service, Incorporated, appellant, versus Michael Andrew Hauck, appellee

   _____

   _____

6. New York Times Company v. L.B. Sullivan

   _____

   _____

7. A Texas Court of Criminal Appeals case, The State of Texas v. Robert Earl Johnson

   _____

   _____

8. South Dakota Department of Health v. Tony Heim

   _____

   _____

9.   In the Matter of Guardian Casualty Company

_____

_____

10.   Tex Smith d/b/a The Harmonica Man versus Arthur Godfrey, et al.

_____

_____

11.   A federal case from the Eastern District of Missouri, The State of
      Missouri ex rel. Wear versus Springfield Gas & Electric Company,
      Incorporated

_____

_____

12.   American Exchange Bank of Madison, Wisconsin versus The United
      States of America

_____

_____

13.   Anna & Henry Carlyle, appellants, versus The United States of
      America, appellee

_____

_____

14.   Columbia Broadcasting System, petitioner, versus The Democratic
      National Committee, respondent [Hint: Columbia Broadcasting System
      is the television network CBS and is commonly referred to by its
      initials.]

_____

_____

15.   Helen Palsgraf, appellant, versus The Long Island Railroad Company,
      appellee

_____

_____

Chapter 2

CASE LOCATION

Now that you know how to begin your legal case citation with the proper case name, you are ready to tackle the second major part of the citation: the case location information. Currently, the most commonly used location information for a case is the case's location in a reporter. In that case, the citation "formula" is one you are already familiar with:

Party 1 v. Party 2, Vol. Reporter Pg. (Court Date).

However, some jurisdictions have adopted location information that references the year of the decision and a number assigned to the case by the court that issued the opinion. That citation format is called "neutral citation." Neutral citations use this formula:

Party 1 v. Party 2, Year COURT No., Vol. Reporter Pg.

You may or may not be able to tell that the comma following the case name in each formula is not italicized. Rule 1.4 tells us to italicize commas that are *within* italicized material but not those that *follow* italicized material. Because the comma after a case name follows italicized material, it is not italicized.

A. Reporters

A "reporter" is a compilation of judicial opinions, or cases. The compilation may be by jurisdiction (*e.g.*, *Florida Reports*) or by subject matter (*e.g.*, *Education Law Reporter*). A given case will be published in the reporter or reporters for that case's jurisdiction and may also appear in a subject matter reporter that contains other cases with the same topic. Legal citation, however, references only jurisdictional reporters.

Jurisdictional reporters may be either official publications of the state or federal government or unofficial publications of private publishers. Both official and unofficial reporters are printed in series. Generally, reporter publishers will begin a new series rather than allow the volume numbers to exceed three digits. Therefore, after volume 999 of *South Western Reporter*, Second Series, the publisher next published volume 1 of *South Western Reporter*, Third Series.

State court cases are published in both state and regional reporters. State reporters may be official or unofficial and contain cases from only one state. Regional reporters are unofficial reporters published by West Group. These reporters contain state court cases from several states. For example, *Southern Reporter* publishes state court cases from Alabama, Florida, Louisiana, and Mississippi.

Federal cases are published in jurisdictional reporters by level of court. Federal district court cases are published in *Federal Supplement*. Federal courts of appeals cases are published in *Federal Reporter*. United States Supreme Court cases are published in three reporters: *United States Reports* (official), *Supreme Court Reporter* (unofficial), and *Lawyers' Edition* (unofficial).

Rules 12.3, 12.4, and 12.5 tell us that a citation must include a volume designation, the abbreviated name of the reporter, and the page on which the opinion begins in the reporter. Appendix 1 of the *ALWD Manual* is a listing of information for each jurisdiction in the United States. The listing first gives state information organized alphabetically by state name and then federal information. The first information given for each jurisdiction is the names of the courts in that jurisdiction, the names of the reporters for each court, and the abbreviations for those reporters.

Placing the volume designation in the citation is straightforward. The volume number appears on the spine of the reporter, and that number is the first information given in the case location portion of the citation.

Placing the reporter information in the citation requires a little more information. The abbreviation for the reporter is in the appropriate jurisdictional section of Appendix 1. Pay special attention to the spacing of the abbreviation. This spacing follows the rules given in 2.2. Rule 2.2 tells us to close up consecutive single capitals (*e.g.*, N.Y.). Ordinals (*e.g.*, 1st, 2d, 4th, etc.) are treated as single capitals (*e.g.*, S.W.2d). Longer abbreviations and single capitals adjacent to longer abbreviations should have a space between them (*e.g.*, Ala.^App. and F.^Supp.).[1] You can combine these spacing rules to handle both adjacent single capitals and longer abbreviations in the same reporter abbreviation (*e.g.*, N.C.^App.).

Finally, the number of the first page that the case appears on in the reporter follows the reporter abbreviation. When you give the reader the initial page number of the case, he or she has the information needed to find the case.

Hunter v. Gatherer, 789 Rptr. 234 (Ct. 2002).

Sometimes, you will also want to direct your reader's attention to specific pages within the case. You can do this using a "pinpoint reference." Rules 12.5(b) and 5.2 say that you can pinpoint the location of specific information by following the initial page number in the citation with a comma, a space, and the page number containing the specific material. This specific page number is included *in addition to* the initial page number rather than as a substitute for it.

Hunter v. Gatherer, 789 Rptr. 234, 237 (Ct. 2002).

If your pinpointed material spans more than one page, Rule 5.3 tells you to give the beginning and ending page numbers, separated by a hyphen or dash.

Tree v. Shrub, 789 Rptr. 85, 87–89 (Ct. 2002).

If the page numbers contain more than two digits, Rule 5.3(b) gives you the option either to retain all digits or to drop repetitive digits except for the last two. Although both are equally correct, the ICW online exercises can only take

---

[1] The caret symbol (^) in these examples shows the location of the space but would not actually be included in your citation.

one correct answer and will follow the convention of retaining all digits on both sides.

Correct: *Hunter v. Gatherer*, 789 Rptr. 234, 237–39 (Ct. 2002).

Correct: *Hunter v. Gatherer*, 789 Rptr. 234, 237–**239** (Ct. 2002). [ICW preferred]

Let's try an example to see how these rules work together. Say we have a Louisiana case called *Red v. Green*. *Red v. Green* is published in the Second Series of the *Southern Reporter*, volume 999, beginning on page 111. First, you know that the volume number goes first. It follows immediately after the case name, separated by a comma and a single space.

Red v. Green, 999

Next comes the reporter. It has to be abbreviated, so we look under the jurisdiction of the case, "Louisiana," in Appendix 1 and find that *Southern Reporter* is abbreviated "So." or "So. 2d" depending on whether the case is printed in the First or Second Series. We know that our volume is in the Second Series, so "So. 2d" it is. Now we check Rule 2.2 to see the proper spacing to use in the abbreviation. "So." is not a single capital and "2d" is an ordinal treated as a single capital. Therefore, Rule 2.2(a) tells you to put a space between them.

Red v. Green, 999 So. 2d

In many reporters, the header of each page contains a notation that reads "Cite as:" followed by the volume, reporter abbreviation, and page number of the case. While you can rely on the given volume and page number, be careful about relying on that header for the reporter abbreviation. The spacing in those abbreviations does not always conform to the *ALWD Manual*. For example, West's *Federal Supplement* headers give "F.Supp." as the appropriate abbreviation. However, Rule 2.2(c) requires a space between "F." and "Supp."

Back to our citation: All we lack is the beginning page number of the case. After we add that, the name and reporter elements of our citation are as follows:

Red v. Green, 999 So. 2d 111

If we were citing to specific pages, 115 through 116, for example, in *Red v. Green*, they would follow the first page of the case. Remember, according to Rule 5.2, we add the specific page to our citation as a pinpoint reference after the page on which our case begins. Remember that when a pinpoint reference spans consecutive pages, you should include the first and last page numbers for the span, separated by a hyphen or dash. Although you may either retain all digits or only the last two, the ICW will be checking for all digits on both sides of the span. Then the name and reporter elements of our citation would be this:

Red v. Green, 999 So. 2d 111, 115–116.

B. Neutral Citation

Rule 12.16 provides an alternative to reporter citations. This alternative is called "neutral citation." Neutral citation format allows citation to the year of the decision, the court's abbreviation, the sequential number of the decision as assigned by the court issuing the opinion, and citation to a reporter.

Party 1 v. Party 2, **Year COURT No., Vol. Reporter Pg.**

Although this is the formula suggested by Rule 12.16(c), individual states may prefer a different format. In that case, we follow that state's local rules for neutral citation.

When a citation to a regional reporter is available, Rule 12.16(c) calls for neutral citation *in addition* to a reporter citation. Otherwise, neutral citation is used alone, without a reporter citation. To determine whether a state requires neutral citation, consult that jurisdiction's information in Appendix 2. Although the *ALWD Manual* does not provide a pinpoint reference format for neutral citations, local rules usually provide the format to be used with that state's opinions.

Drafting neutral citations is pretty simple. Let's say you want to cite *Orange v. Purple*, a North Dakota case decided in 1997. This was the ninety-sixth case decided in 1997 by the North Dakota Court of Appeals. The case is not included in *North Western Reporter*, the regional reporter that includes North Dakota state cases.

First, we look in Appendix 2 under "North Dakota" to see if North Dakota has adopted a public domain format. We find that, for cases decided after January 1, 1997, North Dakota has adopted the neutral citation format suggested by Rule 12.16(c). Therefore, we start with the year of decision:

Orange v. Purple, 1997

Next, we add the court abbreviation for the North Dakota Court of Appeals. North Dakota local rules printed in Appendix 2 call for the North Dakota Courts of Appeals to be abbreviated in neutral citations as "ND App" (without periods).

Orange v. Purple, 1997 ND App

Finally, we add the sequential number of the decision, 96. Because we do not need any more information to make this citation complete, we can place a period at the end of our citation sentence. Notice that this differs from reporter citations in that reporter citations require a court and date parenthetical before they are complete. (Chapter 3 introduces you to the court and date parenthetical.)

Orange v. Purple, 1997 ND App 96.

If you wanted to direct your reader's attention to specific material, you could use a pinpoint reference as directed by the local rules. These rules allow for "spot cites" using the paragraph rather than page numbers of an opinion. Therefore, if the information you wanted to point out is found in the eleventh paragraph of the opinion, you would pinpoint this way:

Orange v. Purple, 1997 ND App 96, ¶ 11.

Checklist for Print Reporters

- Have you put the volume number first?
- Have you abbreviated the reporter name as shown in Appendix 1?
- Have you closed up consecutive single capitals as shown in Rule 2.2?
- Have you given the first page of the case, even if there is also a pinpoint citation?
- Have you checked to make sure you have not put an extra space anywhere?

Checklist for Neutral Citations

- Have you consulted Appendix 2 to see if the case's jurisdiction has adopted neutral citation? If it has, continue. If it has not, give a reporter citation rather than a neutral citation.
- Have you put the year of decision first?
- Have you given the court's abbreviation?
- Have you given the sequential number of the decision?
- If you need to direct your reader to specific material, have you included a pinpoint to the paragraph containing the material?
- Have you placed a period at the end of the citation?

Exercise 2

Case Location

Put the following case name and reporter information or neutral citation information in correct *ALWD* citation form. Do not put a period at the conclusion of the "citation" you draft if a court and date parenthetical would be needed to complete the citation. All cases are being cited in a brief to be filed with the United States Supreme Court. Although this exercise builds on the rules used in the previous exercise, this exercise focuses on Rules 2.2, 12.3, 12.4, 12.5, and 12.16. You will also need to refer to Appendices 1 and 2 for information on reporter abbreviations and neutral citation requirements. If no neutral citation information is given, assume that none is available.

1. Susette Kelo, et al., Petitioners v. City of New London, Connecticut, et al., a United States Supreme Court case reported in volume 545, page 469, of *United States Reports*.

   _____

   _____

2. C.S. Moreland v. Chesapeake Stone Company, a Court of Appeals of Kentucky case reported in volume 104, page 762, of *Southwestern Reporter*.

   _____

   _____

3. 99 Cents Only Stores, a California corporation, versus Lancaster Redevelopment Agency, a public entity, and City of Lancaster, a public entity, a federal district court case published in volume 237, page 1123, of *Federal Supplement*, Second Series.

   _____

   _____

4. Frank E. Midkiff, Richard Lyman, Jr., Hung Wo Ching, Matsuo Takabuki and Myron B. Thompson, Trustees of the Kamehameha Schools/Bishop Estate, Plaintiff-Appellants, versus Paul A. Tom, Tony Taniguchi, Wilbert K. Eguchi, Wahne T. Takahashi, Commissioners of the Hawaii Housing Authority, Defendants-Appellants, a case decided by the United States Court of Appeals for the Ninth Circuit and reported in volume 702, page 788, of *Federal Reporter*, Second Series.

   _____

   _____

5. Michael J. Glick, D.D.S. versus Chocorua Forestlands Limited Partnership, a case decided by the Supreme Court of New Hampshire and reported in volume 949, page 693, of *Atlantic Reporter*, Second Series.

   _____

   _____

6. Nick F. Gyurkey, Plaintiff-Appellant, versus Lloyd Babler, Jr., Thomas Babler, Raymond A. Town, Jr., dba Western International Investors & Development Co., a case decided by the Supreme Court of Idaho and reported in volume 651, page 928, of *Pacific Reporter*.

_____

_____

7. Catherine Johnner versus Percy D. Mims, a case decided by the Supreme Court, Appellate Division, Second Department, of New York and reported in volume 850, page 786, of *New York Supplement*, Second Series.

_____

_____

8. Pacific Scene, Inc., v. Penasquitos, Inc., a case decided by the Supreme Court of California and reported in volume 250, page 651, of *California Reporter*.

_____

_____

9. Robert V. Bolinske, Petitioner, versus Alvin A. Jaeger, Respondent. This is a Supreme Court of North Dakota opinion issued as the 180th opinion of 2008. You may assume that no reporter information is available for this case.

_____

_____

10. Robert David Knight, Plaintiff/Appellant versus Johnny Miller, Defendant/Appellee. This is a Supreme Court of Oklahoma opinion issued as the 81st opinion of 2008. You may assume that no reporter information is available for this case. You wish to direct your reader's attention to specific material in paragraph 3 of the opinion.

_____

_____

Chapter 3

COURT & DATE

Congratulations! Now that you have mastered two major parts of a basic case citation, case names and case location, you are ready to learn the third and final portion of a case citation: the parenthetical containing the court deciding the case and the year of that decision. The court and date parenthetical appears immediately following the page information in your case citation. Now that you have constructed a full citation, you should end it with a period. A case citation used as a separate citation sentence, *i.e.*, not embedded in a textual sentence, should be punctuated as a sentence: Begin with a capital letter and end by placing a period after the court and date parenthetical. The general rules concerning this portion of the citation are Rules 12.6 and 12.7, so you should read these rules carefully before attempting Exercise 3.

Party 1 v. Party 2, Vol. Reporter Pg. (Court Date).

A. Court Information

By looking at a case citation, your reader should be able to determine what court decided the case. In many citations, your reader will be able to make that determination from the reporter information because some official reporters publish only opinions of certain courts. In those citations, you will not include additional information in the court and date parenthetical. For example, *United States Reports* publishes only cases decided by the United States Supreme Court. Therefore, Rule 12.6(d) tells us that a cite to a case published in *United States Reports* can refer only to a United States Supreme Court case. Accordingly, you would not include additional information in the court and date parenthetical.

Boerne v. Flores, 521 U.S. 507 (1997).

1. State Cases

Some states have official reporters that publish only cases decided by a particular court in that state. For parallel citations with these reporters, Rule 12.6(e) provides that no additional information in the court and date parenthetical is necessary. For example, *South Dakota Reports* publishes only cases decided by the South Dakota Supreme Court. Therefore, a cite to a case published in *South Dakota Reports* would not include additional information in the court and date parenthetical because the reporter abbreviation, "S.D.," tells the reader that the South Dakota Supreme Court decided the case.

Landrum v. DeBruycker, 90 S.D. 304, 240 N.W.2d 119 (1976).

However, most reporters, particularly regional reporters, publish opinions from several different state courts. In each of those citations, you must include information telling your reader which court decided the case in question. Rule 12.6(a) and Appendix 1 assist us in formulating the abbreviation for each state court. For example, if you have a case from the Montana Supreme Court, you can look in the Montana entry in Appendix 1 and see that the abbreviation for that court appears in parentheses after the heading "Montana Supreme Court": "Mont." Because the reporter abbreviation "P.2d" does not indicate the court that decided this case, you would include that abbreviation in the court and date parenthetical.

State v. Ommundson, 974 P.2d 620 (Mont. 1999).

Similarly, the *North Western Reporter* publishes cases decided by the highest and intermediate courts in seven different states. Therefore, if you are citing a Michigan Court of Appeals case and are citing to *North Western Reporter*, you would convey the court information to your reader in the court and date parenthetical. You would use the proper abbreviation for the Michigan Court of Appeals that is given in Appendix 1 in the parentheses following the heading "Michigan Court of Appeals": "Mich. App." (We will discuss when a writer needs to cite to a regional reporter and an official state reporter in connection with Exercise 4, Parallel Citations.)

Rutherford v. Chrysler Motors Corp., 231 N.W.2d 413 (Mich. App. 1975).

The *ALWD Manual* also requires that you include information regarding departments, districts, and divisions within state courts. You can find this information in the caption of the case itself.

Kaufman v. Sewerage & Water Bd. of New Orleans, 762 So. 2d 644 (La. App. 4th Cir. 2000).

But wait, there's more! The *ALWD* adds another twist in Rule 12.6(e). Some states publish an official reporter for cases from more than a single court, *e.g.*, from the supreme court and the appellate courts or from different departments or divisions within a certain court. If the name of the reporter tells your reader the name of the state but not the particular court or specific department or division, then you include the additional information in the court and date parenthetical, but omit the state information. For example, if you were going to cite to a New Mexico Court of Appeals case that was reported in *New Mexico Reports*, then you should omit the "N.M." portion of the correct abbreviation "N.M. App."

Lara v. City of Albuquerque, 126 N.M. 455 (App. 1998).

As you might guess, you rarely will have citations like the above example; this situation occurs only when you have a state official reporter that publishes cases from more than one court or when you have a large state with divisions in the court system. Typically, if a state has an official reporter system, only supreme court cases are published or supreme court cases and courts of appeals cases are published in separate reporters. For instance, Washington has two official reporters; *Washington Reports* publishes opinions from the Washington Supreme Court, and *Washington Appellate Reports* publishes opinions from the Washington Court of Appeals.

2. Federal Cases

You must designate a court when citing to any federal case other than a Supreme Court case. The *Federal Reporter* publishes cases from each of the federal courts of appeals. The *Federal Supplement* publishes cases from each United States district court. If you have a case reported in the *Federal Reporter*, you can look under Appendix 4, "Court Abbreviations" and find the heading "United States Courts of Appeals." There you will find abbreviations for each of the circuit courts of appeals: 1st, 2d, 3d, 4th, 5th, 6th, 7th, 8th, 9th, 10th, 11th, D.C. Cir. and Fed. Cir.

Deus v. Allstate Ins. Co., 15 F.3d 506 (5th Cir. 1994).

Pay particular attention to cases decided by the Fifth Circuit in 1981 and 1982. The Fifth Circuit split into the Fifth and Eleventh Circuits on October 1, 1981. Rule 12.6(c) will give you guidance on whether you need additional information in your court and date parenthetical.

If you have a case reported in the *Federal Supplement*, you should look under the heading "United States District Courts" in Appendix 4. Appendix 4 lists the proper abbreviations for all the U.S. District Courts. In case of any confusion, remember that, according to Rule 2.2(a) and 2.2(c), adjacent capitals do not have spaces between them (S.D.N.Y.), but you must put a space between capitals and other abbreviations (D. Mass.).

Jones v. Clinton, 57 F. Supp. 2d 719 (E.D. Ark. 1999).

Bottom line: Your reader must be able to tell what court in what jurisdiction decided a certain case by looking at the citation. Whatever information the name of the reporter does not give, you must include in the court and date parenthetical.

B. Date Information

Your reader also must be able to glean from your citation the date that your case was decided. Please note that the important date is the date the case was *decided*, not the date the case was *argued* or *heard*. For the majority of the cases that you cite, you will know what year the case was decided from reading the heading of the case in a reporter. For these cases, you simply include the year in the court and date parenthetical.

Stein v. Plainwell Community Schs., 822 F.2d 1406 (6th Cir. 1987).

Also, for cases that are not published in a reporter, you will need to include additional information besides the year of decision, according to Rule 12.7(c). For instance, if a case is not reported or is reported in a slip opinion or an electronic database, then you must give the exact date, *i.e.*, month, day, and year, of the decision. Note that Appendix 3 provides the proper abbreviations for the months of the year.

Checklist for Court Information

- Are you citing from a federal reporter, a regional reporter, or a state reporter?
- If a federal reporter, but not *United States Reports*, have you included an abbreviation for the deciding court as shown in Appendix 4?
- If a regional reporter, have you included a full abbreviation for the deciding court as shown in Appendix 1?
- Does your state court have any division or department information that should be included?
- If a state reporter, does the state reporter publish opinions from any other court besides the deciding court?
- If the state reporter does publish opinions from more than one court, have you included an abbreviation for the deciding court as shown in Appendix 1? Do you need to include the part of the abbreviation designating the name of the state, or an you omit that information?
- Have you double-checked the spacing of your abbreviation according to Rule 2.2(a) and Rule 2.2(c)?

Checklist for Date Information

- Is your case decided in a reporter? If so, have you included the year of decision in your citation?
- If your case is not reported in print, have you included the month, day, and year in your citation?

Exercise 3

Court & Date

Put the following information in correct *ALWD* citation form. All cases are being cited in citation sentences. Although this exercise builds on the rules used in the previous exercise, this exercise focuses on Rules 12.6 and 12.7. You will also need to refer to Chart 12.1 for information on the reporters, and Appendices 1 and 4 for information on the abbreviations of courts.

1. George Hawkins versus Edward R. B. McGee, a case from the Supreme Court of New Hampshire, decided June 4, 1929, and reported at volume 146, page 641, of *Atlantic Reporter*.

   _____

   _____

2. Willie Peevyhouse and Lucille Peevyhouse versus Garland Coal & Mining Company, a case decided by the Supreme Court of Oklahoma on December 11, 1962, and reported at volume 382, page 109, of *Pacific Reporter*, Second Series.

   _____

   _____

3. Steven Merola versus Exergen Corporation and Francesco Pompei, a case decided by the Appeals Court of Massachusetts on April 26, 1995, after argument on February 16, 1995, and reported at volume 648, page 1301, of *North Eastern Reporter*, Second Series.

   _____

   _____

4. Warner-Lambert Pharmaceutical Company, Inc. versus John J. Reynolds, Inc., et al., a case decided by the United States District Court in the Southern District of New York on November 6, 1959, and reported at volume 178, page 655, of *Federal Supplement*.

   _____

   _____

5. Sally Beauty Company, Inc., versus Nexxus Products Company, Inc., a case decided by the United States Court of Appeals for the Seventh Circuit on September 26, 1986, and reported at volume 801, page 1001, of *Federal Reporter*, Second Series.

   _____

   _____

6. Jerome D. Salinger a/k/a J.D. Salinger versus Random House, Inc. and Ian Hamilton, a case decided by the United States Court of Appeals for the First Circuit on January 29, 1987, and reported at volume 811, page 90, of *Federal Reporter*, Second Series.

7. Andrew D. Ricketts versus Katie Scothorn, a case decided by the Supreme Court of Nebraska on December 8, 1898, and reported at volume 77, page 365, of *North Western Reporter*.

8. General Utilities & Operating Company versus the Commission of Internal Revenue, Guy T. Helvering, a case decided by the United States Supreme Court in 1935 and reported at volume 296, page 200, of *United States Reports*.

9. Marion E. Seaver versus Matt C. Ransom, executor, a case decided by the New York Court of Appeals on October 1, 1918, and reported at volume 120, page 639, of *North Eastern Reporter*.

10. Frank Floyd, et al. versus Billy Watson, et al., a case decided by the Supreme Court of Appeals in West Virginia on May 15, 1979, and reported at volume 254, page 687, of *South Eastern Reporter*, Second Series. You want to focus the reader's attention on material located on page 689.

Chapter 4

PARALLEL CITATIONS

Now that you have mastered the basic citation, you are ready to add a twist. The first thing we will add is the parallel citation. You learned from the previous exercises that some states have their opinions published in their own official reporter (referred to throughout this chapter as the state reporter) as well as the appropriate unofficial reporter published by West Group (referred to throughout this chapter as the regional reporter). For example, opinions from the Idaho Supreme Court and Idaho Court of Appeals are published in both *Idaho Reports* and *Pacific Reporter*. When you cite opinions from such a state to a court in that state, and when local rules of citation require it, Rule 12.4(c) calls for a citation to both the official and unofficial reporters. Remember also that some states have adopted neutral citation according to Rule 12.16 for citations to that state's opinions. When citing to decisions from those states to those states' courts, Rule 12.16 and many local rules require a neutral citation and a regional reporter citation.

However, if you are citing in a document to be filed with a federal court or a court outside the state in which the case was decided, Rule 12.4(a)(2) requires that you cite to only the regional reporter. Before you begin the Parallel Citations exercise, read Rules 12.4 and 12.6(3) and Sidebars 12.4 and 12.5 carefully.

The first decision you have to make is whether you need a parallel citation. If your case is from a federal court, you will not parallel cite. This rule extends to United States Supreme Court cases as well. Even though they are published in *United States Reports, Supreme Court Reporter,* and *Lawyers' Edition*, Rule 12.4(b) tells you to cite to only *United States Reports*.

A. States Not Requiring Neutral Citation

If your case is from a state that has its own reporter and you are citing this case in a document to a state court in that state, you will *usually* cite both the state and the regional reporters. The *ALWD Manual* directs you to first consult Appendix 2 for the local rules that tell whether a given state requires parallel citation. If local rules do require citation to more than one reporter, you will then use Appendix 1 in much the same way you do for any citation.

First, determine the jurisdiction of the case. Next, look up that jurisdiction in Appendix 1. Appendix 1 will tell you which reporters to cite and how those reporters are abbreviated. Rule 12.4(c)(3) gives the appropriate order for listing reporters in a parallel citation. Usually, you will have only one official state reporter and the unofficial West regional reporter. In that case, list the state reporter first. If you have anything other than a state and regional reporter, consult 12.4(c)(3) for the appropriate order of sources in the citation. Remember that some cases are printed in many different sources besides just state and regional reporters. Some publishers print subject matter reporters, compiling all the opinions in a certain subject area into one reporter. Also, some secondary research sources, such as *American Law Reports* (A.L.R.), publish the full text of opinions related to the articles they publish. Regardless of the number of publications in which your case is published, you will only cite to the reporters required by Appendix 2 and listed in Appendix 1.[1]

The next decision with a parallel citation is whether and how to identify the court that issued the opinion. Remember that the general rule, according to Rule 12.6(a)(2), is that you do include the court abbreviation. Abbreviations for state courts can be found in each state's section of Appendix 1. Abbreviations for federal courts can be found in Appendix 4. The exception to 12.6(a)(2) is familiar to you from 12.4(c)(3) — a rule you used in the Chapter 3 exercise. This rule, repeated in 12.6(e), allows you to drop all or part of the court abbreviation if that part of the court abbreviation is obvious from one of the reporter abbreviations.

Lukowsky v. Shalit, 487 **N.Y.** S. 2d 781 (**App. Div.** 1985).

Remembering these rules might be easier if you know the rationale behind them. The basic rationale behind every citation rule is to keep the citation as short as possible while still conveying all significant information. This is why we generally include only the state and regional reporter and not every possible source that might publish an opinion. Likewise, why include the court abbreviation if it is obvious from the name of the reporter? Wait a minute . . . if brevity is so important, then why use a parallel citation at all? The answer is "convenience." Some practitioners and courts will subscribe only to the state reporter, usually because of financial or shelf-space constraints. A parallel citation helps people using only the state reporter from having to resort to a cross-reference index each time they want to look up a case.[2]

Let's try an example to see how these rules work. Suppose you are going to cite the Georgia Supreme Court case *Black v. Blue* in a brief you will file with the Georgia Court of Appeals. This is a 1972 case that is reported at volume 321, page 543, of *Georgia Reports*, Georgia's official state reporter. This opinion is also reported at volume 76, page 123, of *South Eastern Reporter*, Second Series. *South Eastern Reporter* is the unofficial West regional reporter that includes Georgia state cases.

---

[1] Do not be fooled by citations you read in reported cases! For example, opinions published in the West regional reporter system often contain parallel citations to other subject matter reporters published by West. These types of parallel citations do not conform to the *ALWD Manual* and should not be copied into your own writing.

[2] To accommodate lawyers and judges who need only a single state's case law, West publishes "offprints." You have probably noticed the reference in Appendix 1 to "West offprints." For example, in the Georgia section, after "South Eastern Reporter," you see a reference to "Georgia Cases (West offprint)." The West offprints are reporter volumes that include only the cases from a given state. For example, *South Eastern Reporter* contains cases from several states in addition to Georgia. However, practitioners in Georgia may only need the Georgia cases included in *South Eastern Reporter*. In that case, they can buy a version of *South Eastern Reporter* that contains only the cases from Georgia. This would be called the *Georgia Cases* (West offprint) of *South Eastern Reporter*. The citations in Georgia Cases are identical to those in *South Eastern Reporter*. Therefore, a parallel citation to both the regional reporter and the West offprint would be redundant and unnecessary.

Let's get the easy part of the citation out of the way first. We know we can start with the case name:

Black v. Blue,

Now, let's tackle the first decision: whether to include a parallel citation. This is a Georgia case, and we will be citing it to a Georgia court.

Remember that you want to first consult the local rules for the court the document will be submitted to in order to determine whether a parallel citation is required. Because we will be citing this case to the Georgia Court of Appeals, we first go to the Georgia section of Appendix 2. In that section, we find that citations of Georgia cases to Georgia courts must include the volume and page number of the official Georgia reporter. This means that Georgia requires a parallel citation to the official state reporter as well as the standard citation to the unofficial regional reporter. Unless specifically instructed otherwise, you can assume that local rules requiring citation to the state reporter intend for you to cite the state reporter *in addition* to the regional reporter.

Although you will use Appendix 2 to determine which reporters to cite, you will consult Appendix 1 for the appropriate abbreviations for those reporters. Turning to the Georgia section of Appendix 1, we find that the official reporter is *Georgia Reports* and is abbreviated "Ga."; the unofficial reporter is *South Eastern Reporter,* and its Second Series is abbreviated "S.E.2d." So, those reporter abbreviations will be as follows:

321 Ga. 543

76 S.E.2d 123

Now that we have completed the first step, deciding which reporters to include and how to cite those reporters, we are ready for Step 2: determining in which order to place the reporters. For that, we will turn to Rule 12.4(c)(3), which tells us that we should cite official reporters before unofficial reporters. Therefore, *Georgia Reports*, the official reporter, will be listed first. So, here we go!

Black v. Blue, 321 Ga. 543, 76 S.E.2d 123

Finally, Step 3 is deciding what to include for the court abbreviation in the court and date parenthetical. Turning to the Georgia section of Appendix 1, we find that the Georgia Supreme Court is abbreviated "Ga." Because "Ga." is also the abbreviation for the official reporter, the jurisdiction of the case will be obvious from the reporter abbreviation, and Rule 12.6(e) tells us that we do not have to repeat that information in the parenthetical. So, we will just add the year of the decision and a period, and we are done!

Black v. Blue, 321 Ga. 543, 76 S.E.2d 123 (1972).

Got it? Okay, now take a deep breath, and let's try the same citation in a court document filed with a federal court or a state court outside of Georgia that would not require a parallel cite for a Georgia case. In both of those cases, Rule 12.4(a)(2) requires that we only cite the unofficial West regional reporter. So the first thing we'll do is delete the citation to *Georgia Reports*.

Black v. Blue, 76 S.E.2d 123

Next, let's decide how to identify the court in the court and date parenthetical. Remember that Rule 12.6(a)(2) requires a court abbreviation unless the name of the court is obvious from the reporter abbreviation. Because *South Eastern Reporter* publishes cases from many states, the reporter abbreviation is not sufficient to identify the court. Therefore, we must include the abbreviation for the Georgia Supreme Court — we found that abbreviation, "Ga.," earlier in Georgia's section of Appendix. 1.

Black v. Blue, 76 S.E.2d 123 (Ga. 1972).

Finish it off with the year of decision and a period at the end of our citation sentence, and we are done!

Black v. Blue, 76 S.E.2d 123 (Ga. 1972).

B. States Requiring Neutral Citation

Remember from Chapter 2 that Appendix 2 tells which states require neutral citation. If a state does require neutral citation, Rule 12.16 and many local rules require a parallel citation including a neutral citation and a regional reporter citation. If you give a parallel citation that includes a neutral citation, Rule 12.16 does not require a court and date parenthetical. The reason for omitting the parenthetical is that the information that would ordinarily be in that parenthetical — state abbreviation, court abbreviation, and year of decision — is all included in the neutral citation. Therefore, a court and date parenthetical is unnecessary.

Let's run through an example of a parallel citation that includes neutral citation. Suppose we want to cite the Oklahoma Supreme Court case *Decorte v. Robinson*. This is a 1998 opinion that was issued as the 87th case by the court that year. The case is reported at volume 969, page 358 of *Pacific Reporter*, Second Series. *Pacific Reporter* is the regional reporter that includes Oklahoma state cases.

The first decision is whether our citation should include a neutral citation. To find this out, we check Oklahoma's section of Appendix 2 and find that Oklahoma has adopted the neutral citation format suggested by Rule 12.16. Therefore, we include both the neutral citation and a citation to the regional reporter. Let's start with the neutral citation. The first piece of information required is the year of decision.

Decorte v. Robinson, 1998

Next, we add the neutral citation court abbreviation for the Oklahoma Supreme Court:

Decorte v. Robinson, 1998 OK

Finally, we add the sequential number of the case that was assigned by the court.

Decorte v. Robinson, 1998 OK 87

Now, let's add the citation for the regional reporter. We find the abbreviation for *Pacific Reporter*, Second Series (P.2d), in the Oklahoma section of Appendix 1. Because the reporter abbreviation contains only consecutive single capitals, Rule 2.2(a) tells us to close up all letters in the abbreviation.

Decorte v. Robinson, 1998 OK 87, 969 P.2d 358

Because neither Rule 12.16 nor Oklahoma local rules require a court and date parenthetical with neutral citations, all we have to do is add a period to our citation sentence, and we're done!

Checklist for Parallel Citations

- Are you citing a state case?

    - If not, do not worry about parallel citation.
    - If so, are you citing the case to a state court in that same state?

        - If not, do not worry about parallel citation.
        - If so, turn to that state's section of Appendix 2 to determine whether that state has adopted neutral citation.

- If the state has **not** adopted neutral citation . . .

    - have you used Appendix 2 and Appendix 1 to determine which reporters to cite and how to abbreviate them?
    - have you listed state reporter(s) before the regional reporter?
    - have you placed the court and date parenthetical at the end of the citation as per Rule 12?
    - have you included a court abbreviation in the court and date parenthetical only if the name of the court is not obvious from the reporter abbreviation?

- If the state **has** adopted neutral citation . . .

    - have you listed the neutral citation first?
    - have you included the citation to the regional reporter if one is available?
    - have you omitted the court and date parenthetical?

- If the state has adopted a neutral citation format that differs from Rule 12.16, have you consulted local rules for the format and information to include?

Exercise 4

Parallel Citations

Put the following information in correct *ALWD* citation form. All cases are being cited in citation sentences. Although this exercise builds on the rules used in previous exercises, this exercise focuses on Rules 12.4 and 12.6(e). You will also need to refer to Appendix 2 for information on which reporters to cite and Appendix 1 for reporter abbreviations. Do not include neutral citation unless local rules in Appendix 2 require it.

1. In a brief filed with the Supreme Court of Virginia, you cite the 1912 Supreme Court of Appeals of West Virginia case Lyons versus Fairmont Real Estate Co. The case is reported in volume 71, page 754, of *West Virginia Reports* and in volume 77, page 525, of *South Eastern Reporter.*

_____

_____

2. In a brief to the United States Supreme Court, you cite the 1950 Supreme Court of Oklahoma case West Edmond Salt Water Disposal Association versus L.T. Rosecrans, et al. This case is reported in volume 204, page 9, of *Oklahoma Reports* and in volume 226, page 965, of *Pacific Reporter*, Second Series. No local rule governs citation of state court cases to the United States Supreme Court.

_____

_____

3. In a brief to the Fourteenth District Court of Appeals in Texas, you cite the 1983 Supreme Court of Texas case Earl Gooden, et al., Appellants, versus Eugene Tips, M.D., Appellee. The case is reported in volume 651, page 364, of *South Western Reporter*, Second Series, and in volume 43, page 139, of *American Law Reports*, Fourth Series. The State of Texas ceased publication of its state reporter in 1962.

_____

_____

4. In a brief to the Supreme Court of Arkansas, you cite the September 23, 1985, Supreme Court of Arkansas case Grain Dealers Mutual Insurance Company, Appellant versus Helen Porterfield, Appellee. This case is reported in volume 287, page 27, of *Arkansas Reports*; in volume 695, page 833, of *South Western Reporter*, Second Series; and in volume 27, page 977, of *Education Law Reports.*

_____

_____

5. In a brief to the Supreme Court of Oregon, you cite the 1985 Supreme
    Court of Washington case Larry Daugert, Trustee for David M. Simms &
    Gail Simms versus John D. Pappas & Betty Pappas. This case is reported
    in volume 104, page 254, of *Washington Reports*, Second Series, and in
    volume 704, page 600, of *Pacific Reporter*, Second Series.

6. In a brief filed with the Texas Court of Criminal Appeals, you cite the
    1965 Supreme Court of Mississippi case Carl Murphy, Jr. versus State of
    Mississippi. The case is reported in volume 253, page 644, of *Mississippi
    Reports*, and in volume 178, page 692, of *Southern Reporter*, Second
    Series.

7. In a brief to the United States Supreme Court, you cite the 1985 Court of
    Appeals of Maryland case Olen J. Kelley, et ux. versus R.G. Industries,
    Inc., et al. This case is reported in volume 54, page 2195, of *United States
    Law Week*; in volume 44, page 563, of *American Law Reports*, Fourth
    Series; in volume 497, page 1143, of *Atlantic Reporter*, Second Series;
    and in volume 304, page 124, of *Maryland Reports*. No local rules govern
    the citation of state cases to the United States Supreme Court.

8. In a brief filed with the Nebraska Supreme Court, you cite the 1999
    Supreme Court of Nebraska case Ann Kennedy Elsome, appellee, versus
    Paul T. Elsome, appellant. The case is reported in volume 257, page 889,
    of *Nebraska Reports*, and in volume 601, page 537, of *North Western
    Reporter*, Second Series.

9. In a brief filed with the South Dakota Supreme Court, you cite the 2008
    South Dakota Supreme Court case Lorraine Kirksey versus Dorothy E.
    Grohmann. This case is reported in volume 754, page 825, of *North
    Western Reporter*, Second Series. This case was given the sequential
    number of 76 by the South Dakota Supreme Court.

10. In a brief filed with the Montana Supreme Court, you cite the 2008 Montana Supreme Court case Rodney Barnard, Petitioner, versus Liberty Northwest Insurance Corporation, respondent. This case is reported in volume 189, page 1196, of *Pacific Reporter*, Third Series. It was given the sequential number of 254 by the Montana Supreme Court.

_____

_____

Chapter 5

SHORT FORMS (CASES)

Frequently, you will wish to refer to one case several times within a legal memorandum or a court document. Just to prove to you that the *ALWD Manual* does indeed have a heart, you need only give the full legal citation for a case the *first* time you cite to that case. Citing a case in full after having mentioned the case before will, in fact, confuse your reader. Your reader may think you are introducing a new case into your analysis. For all subsequent cites to that case, you will use a short form citation, as long as all subsequent cites are within the same general discussion. Rules 11.2, 11.3, and 12.21 provide information on short form citations for cases. You should read each of those sections carefully before attempting Exercise 5.

The *ALWD Manual* provides two types of short forms to be used for cases in legal memoranda and court documents: "*id.*" and an abbreviated version of the full legal citation. These two types are not interchangeable, but can each be used only in certain instances. (Note that "*supra*" may also be used as a permissible short form for some types of sources. However, according to Rule 11.4(b)(4), "*supra*" is not a permissible short form for cases or statutes.)

Rule 11.3 explains the short form "*id.*" in detail and gives good examples.[1] The short form "*id.*" may be used only when you wish to cite to a case that is cited in the *immediately preceding citation.* In other words, no intervening cites to a different authority of any type should appear between the preceding citation to this case and the current citation. However, the preceding citation to the case may be a full citation or a short form citation, even another "*id.*" designation. Note, however, that simply mentioning a case name in a previous sentence will not support an "*id.*" citation. In addition, the prior citation need only be to the same case, not to the same page in the same case. If you wish to cite to the same page of the same case, then use only the word "*id.*" If you wish to cite to a different page or pages of the same case, but also those page numbers immediately preceded by the word "at."

> Prior to being arrested, Mrs. Jones had accumulated over 100 speeding tickets. *State v. Jones*, 16 Rptr. 33, 34 (St. Ct. 1999). The majority of these tickets listed her speed as at least 20 miles per hour over the posted speed limit. *Id.* Five of the speeding tickets were issued in connection with traffic accidents. *Id.* at 35.

---

[1] "Id." is an abbreviation for "idem," a latin word meaning "the same." It is not capitalized unless it begins a citation sentence. The period following the abbreviation is italicized, as provided in Rule 11.3 (c). In your earlier studies prior to law school, you may have used "Ibid.," which is an abbreviation for the Latin word "ibidem," which means "the same place." For whatever reason, legal writing has developed using only "id."

Two more details to remember: If the immediately preceding citation is a "string cite," *i.e.*, contains more than one authority, then you may not use "*id.*," even if one of those authorities is the case you currently wish to cite. Consider the following three cites that appear consecutively in a paragraph.

State v. Jones, 16 Rptr. 33, 34 (St. Ct. 1999).

Id.; *State v. Smith*, 19 Rptr. 389, 390–392 (St. Ct. 2002).

Smith, 19 Rptr. at 390–92.

The second citation is a string cite referring to both *Jones* and *Smith*. Because *Jones* was the immediately preceding citation, "*id.*" clearly refers to that case. "*Id.*" may be the first part of a string cite. However, notice that the third citation, a reference to *Smith*, is not "*id.*" even though *Smith* is part of the immediately preceding citation. This is because "*id.*" cannot be used to refer to a single source within a string cite. When you think about it, this makes sense. If the second citation above were followed by "*id.*" the reader would likely think you intended a citation to both of the sources in the string cite.

When circumstances do not allow you to use "*id.*," Rule 12.21(b) and (c) provide for the use of an abbreviated short form to refer to previous citations to cases. The *ALWD Manual* provides a very practical system for constructing short forms for cases. According to Rule 12.21(c), if you have referred to the case by name in your textual sentence, the short form to use in your citation sentence will consist only of the volume number, the reporter abbreviation, and the page number, preceded by the word "at." You drop the court and date parenthetical completely. Therefore, the short form for *Tortoise v. Hare*, 467 N.2d 1 (Ct. 2000), in that situation would be as follows:

> In the case mentioned previously, *Tortoise v. Hare*, the plaintiff sued on the theory of breach of an implied contract. 467 N.2d at 3.

If, however, you have not referred to the case by name in that specific textual sentence, then the appropriate short form to use, according to Rule 12.21(b), will retain one party's name.

> In the case mentioned previously, *Tortoise v. Hare*, the plaintiff sued on the theory of breach of an implied contract. 467 N.2d at 3. The facts in this case are similar to the facts of a more recent case, in which the plaintiff also alleged an implied contract. *Androcles v. Lion*, 352 N.2d 54 (Ct. App. 2007). In both cases, the plaintiff prevailed at trial. *Id.* at 59; *Tortoise*, 467 N.2d at 7.

Rule 12.21(b)(3) strongly suggests retaining the first party's name instead of the second party's name unless such use will be confusing. For example, you would not choose the name of a party that is frequently named in litigation, such as a state, the United States, a governmental agency, or the head of an agency or branch of government of either a state or the United States. In addition, Rule 12.21(b)(5) suggests shortening a party's name if the name is long. Therefore, for the case *State v. Roach*, 772 A.2d 395 (N.J. 2001), you would choose as your short form.

Roach, 772 A.2d at 400.

NOT:

State, 772 A.2d at 400.

If the full citation of your case is a parallel citation with two or more reporter references, then craft your abbreviated short form in accordance with Rule 12.21(f). (The authors believe that the option presented in Rule 12.21(f) as "short citation option two" is the most widely accepted form, so the ICW follows this format.) Again, you would drop the first page on which your case appears in each reporter and the court and date parenthetical, but include the relevant page information for each reporter preceded by the word "at."

Roach, 167 N.J. at 600, 772 A.2d at 400.

For the use of "*id.*" with a parallel citation, Rule 12.21(f)(1) allows you to substitute "*id.*" for the official state reporter information in the first part of your citation.

Id. at 600, 772 A.2d at 400.

Lastly, Rule 12.21(b)(2) gives insight to a question we hear from our students fairly often: How do I cite to a case *generally*, *i.e.*, without a pinpoint, in a short form? According to the *ALWD Manual*, you omit "at" and just include the first page of the case, but no court and date parenthetical.

Roach, 772 A.2d 395.

Checklist for Case Short Forms

- Did you cite to the current case in the immediately preceding citation? If so, use "*id.*" If not, then you cannot use "*id.*" and must use an abbreviated short form.

- Does the immediately preceding citation contain more than one authority, *i.e.*, is it a string cite? If so, then you cannot use "*id.*" and must use an abbreviated short form.

- If you cannot use "*id.*," have you formulated an acceptable abbreviated short form?

- In your abbreviated short form, have you retained the volume and reporter name from the full legal citation?

- If the full citation contained a parallel citation, have you included references to both reporters in the short form?

- In your abbreviated short form, have you used the word "at" and a pinpoint page number?

Exercise 5
Short Forms (Cases)

Put the following information in correct *ALWD* citation form. All cases are being cited in citation sentences in text, not footnotes. Although this exercise builds on the rules used in previous exercises, this exercise focuses on Rules 11 and 12.21. In composing the short forms of party names, be guided by the information in each citation problem and assume that no part of the case name has been included in the textual sentence preceding unless specifically told that information. Rule 5.3(b) allows writers to construct pinpoints that refer to consecutive pages in two ways. For consistency, these exercises anticipate answers in which cites to consecutive pages retain all digits on both sides of the span. In addition, Rule 12.21(f) provides two versions for short forms of cases with parallel citations when the case is the immediately preceding source. Use the format listed as the preferred format.

1. In the immediately preceding sentence of a legal memorandum, without an intervening cite, you cited to *Mitsubishi Motors Corp. v. Soler Chrysler-Plymouth, Inc.*, 473 U.S. 614 (1985). You wish to cite to page 616 of the case.

_____

_____

2. Two paragraphs later, after citing to other cases and a statute, you wish to cite to page 616 of *Mitsubishi Motors Corp. v. Soler Chrysler-Plymouth, Inc.*, 473 U.S. 614 (1985), again. You have referred to this case in your textual sentence as *"Mitsubishi Motors."*

_____

_____

3. On page 3 of your legal memorandum, you cited to *Natl. Iranian Oil Co. v. Ashland Oil, Inc.*, 817 F.2d 326 (5th Cir. 1987). On page 6, you would like to cite to National Iranian Oil again, only you would like to focus your reader's attention on information beginning on page 328 and continuing on page 329. You have cited to other cases on pages 4 and 5 of your memorandum. You have not referred to the case by name in your textual sentence, but elsewhere you have referred to the case as *"National Iranian Oil."*

_____

_____

4. In the next sentence, you would like to cite to the same information again. No intervening cites appear between the citation in #3 and the current cite.

_____

_____

5. In the same legal memorandum, you again wish to refer to *Mitsubishi Motors Corp. v. Soler Chrysler-Plymouth, Inc.*, 473 U.S. 614 (1985), focusing your reader's attention on information on page 617. The immediately preceding citation sentence reads "*Mitsubishi Motors*, 473 U.S. at 617; *Natl. Iranian Oil Co. v. Ashland Oil, Inc.*, 817 F.2d 326 (5th Cir. 1987)." Draft the appropriate short form. You have not referred to the case by name in your textual sentence, but elsewhere you have referred to the case as "*Mitsubishi Motors.*"

---

6. In a brief to a New York court, you have previously cited to *Mobil Oil Indon. Inc. v. Asamera (Indon.) Ltd.*, 56 A.D.2d 339, 392 N.Y.S.2d 614 (1977). You wish to cite to *Mobil Oil* again after several intervening cites, focusing your reader on information contained at 56 A.D.2d 341 and 392 N.Y.S.2d 616, respectively. You have not referred to the case by name in your textual sentence.

---

7. In the next sentence, without any intervening cites, you would like to cite to *Mobil Oil* again, only this time you would like to direct your reader's attention to information found at 56 A.D.2d 342 and 392 N.Y.S.2d 617. You have not referred to the case by name in your textual sentence.

---

8. On page 68 of a brief to the Fifth Circuit Court of Appeals, you cite to *U.S. v. Lipshy*, 492 F. Supp. 35 (N.D. Tex. 1979). On page 82 of your brief, you would like to refer to this case again, focusing your reader's attention on information beginning on page 37 and continuing on page 38. You have cited to other cases in the interim. You have not referred to the case by name in your textual sentence.

---

9. You wish to formulate a short form, not "*id.*," for information found on the first page of *Katzenbach v. McClung*, 379 U.S. 294 (1964). You have not referred to the case by name in the textual sentence. [*Hint: Nicholas Katzenbach was the acting Attorney General of the United States and was named in many civil rights cases during that time.*]

---

10. You wish to formulate a short form, not "*id.*," for information found on page 428 and continuing on page 429 of *Bunge v. First Natl. Bank of Mount Holly Springs, P.A.*, 118 F.2d 427 (3d Cir. 1941). You have not referred to the case by name in your textual sentence.

_____

_____

Chapter 6

FEDERAL STATUTES

The general rules for citing federal statutes are located in Chapter 14 of the *ALWD Manual*. The rules relating to rules of procedure and rules of evidence, which are codified with the federal statutes, appear in a separate chapter, Chapter 17. Citation of the United States Constitution is the subject of Chapter 13. You will also need to be familiar with Rule 6 for section symbols and spacing.

Both the federal statutes and the United States Constitution are published in an official compilation, the *United States Code*. Although technically not statutes, the United States Constitution and federal rules of procedure and evidence are also published in the *United States Code*. The *United States Code* is divided into subject matter areas called "titles." Each title is numbered and may span more than one hard-bound volume. Within each title, each statute is given a section number and may be divided into subsections. If possible, always cite the *United States Code*, which is the official code. Otherwise, you may cite to the *United States Code Annotated* or the *United States Code Service*.

To get a start on federal statutory citation form, look at the citations analyzed in Rule 14.2 of the *ALWD Manual*. The basic "formula" for a federal statute citation follows:

Title U.S.C. § Section (Date).

Rule 14.2(g) tells us that we may include the name of the act, but the name is not mandatory. If included, the name of the act appears in ordinary type at the beginning of the statute, similar to the name of a case.

Clean Water Act, 33 U.S.C. § 1314(a)(1) (2006).

The first required component of the citation is the title number, which is analogous to a case citation's volume number. In a federal statutory citation, the title number precedes the name of the code cited just as the volume number of a case reporter precedes the name of the reporter in a case citation. The section number follows the abbreviated code just as the page number follows the abbreviated reporter name in a case citation:

123 U.S. 456

28 U.S.C. § 1291

You cite individual code sections by using a single section symbol (§) followed by the section number. Rule 6.2 tells you to insert a space between the section symbol and the section number. To indicate that you are citing to more than one numbered section, use a double section symbol (§§) followed by a space and the section numbers. Rule 6.6(a) tells you to indicate a span of consecutive sections or subsections by using a hyphen between the inclusive numbers. To cite to nonconsecutive sections or subsections, use a comma and a space to separate the section numbers.

28 U.S.C. §§ 1331–1367, 1441–1452 (2006).

28 U.S.C. §§ 1331, 1441 (2006).

Note, however, that you do not use double section symbols when you are citing to multiple subsections within the same numbered section.

28 U.S.C. § 1367(a)–(b) (2006).

When citing multiple subsubsections of a statute, you will generally follow the same rules as those for citing sections. When dealing with subsubsections, you will not repeat digits or letters.

28 U.S.C. § 105(b)(1), (5)

19 U.S.C. § 1490(a)(1)(A)–(C)

NOT:

28 U.S.C. § 105(b)(1), (b)(5)

19 U.S.C. § 1490(a)(1)(A)–(a)(1)(C)

Look again at the full citations given above. The last element in each is a year in parentheses. Rule 14.2(f) governs the insertion of the date in your citation. The U.S.C. main volumes are published every six years. The code is kept up to date between complete publications by annual supplements. When you are research-ing and citing federal statutes, you must make sure that the statutory provisions you are using and citing are the ones currently in effect.

If all of your cited material appears in the main volume, then you simply include the year the main volume was published. If all of your cited material appears in a supplement, then you indicate this by including the abbreviation "Supp." and the year the supplement was published. If your reader would need to consult both the main volume and a supplement, then you must include both pieces of information, connected by an ampersand (&).

Title U.S.C. § Section (Year & Supp. Year).

Let's walk through a federal statutory citation to get you started. Let's put section 501 of title 17 of the *United States Code* into a citation sentence. Subsection (a) of the statute is in the 2004 Supplement, but all remaining provisions are in the main volume, published in 2000. We are not using the name of the act of which this statute is a part, so you know from Rule 14.2(a) that the first element of a federal statutory citation is the number of the title. In our statute that number is 17. Next is the abbreviation of the code. Following the information on federal courts, Appendix 1 shows the proper abbreviations and formats for "Statutory compilations." You see that the abbreviation for the *United States Code* is "U.S.C." Rule 2.2(a) tells you to close up adjacent single capitals, so make sure there are no spaces in "U.S.C."

17 U.S.C.

Next comes a section symbol followed by a space. After the section symbol and space, you will insert the section number. In this example, assume that also wish to cite to a subsection, (c). Rule 6.4(b) tells you to use the original punctuation (meaning the punctuation used in the code itself) dividing sections from subsections. Therefore, our complete statute number is 501(c). Note that no spaces are inserted between the main section and the subsection.

17 U.S.C. § 501(c)

The final element is the year. You already know that the statute is currently in force and that you are citing the official code. Therefore, according to Rule 14.2(e), you do not have to show the name of a publisher. You know also that the main volumes of the current official code were published in 2000, and the supplement was published in 2004.

17 U.S.C. § 501(c) (2000 & Supp. 2004).

In addition to these rules for citing most statutes, you do need to know some rules for some specific statutes. For example, Rule 14.2(b)(3) tells you that when citing to the Internal Revenue Code, you may cite to "I.R.C." rather than to title 26 of the *United States Code.*

I.R.C. § 703(a) (2006).

NOT:

26 U.S.C. § 703(a) (2006).

In addition, Rule 17.1 tells us that cites to the current version of certain rules, such as the Federal Rules of Civil Procedure, which are published in an appendix to the *United States Code,* do not cite to the *United States Code,* but instead cite only to the rules themselves. A citation to the current version of the rule does not require a date parenthetical. Although Appendix 3 gives two acceptable abbreviations for "procedure" ("P." and "Proc."), the examples indicate a preference for "P." when citing rules of procedure.

Fed. R. Civ. P. 26(b)(4).

Checklist for Federal Statutes

- If you are using the name of the statute, have you put that name first in ordinary type?
- Have you put the title number before the name of the code?
- Have you properly abbreviated the name of the code?
- Have you closed up (left no spaces between) all adjacent single capitals in the abbreviated name of the code?
- Have you inserted a single section symbol for a single statute and a double section symbol for more than one statute?
- Have you left a single space between the section symbol and the section number?
- Have you closed up the section number and its subsections?
- Have you put the year(s) of publication in parentheses at the end of your citation?
- If any portion of your cited material is included in a supplementary volume, have you indicated this in the date parenthetical?
- Have you left a space between the last character of the section number and the date parenthetical?
- Have you ended your citation sentence with a period?

Exercise 6

Federal Statutes

Put the following information in correct *ALWD* citation form. All statutes are being cited in citation sentences. This exercise focuses on Rules 13.1 through 14.2(f) and 17.1 through 17.1(c).

1. The eleventh amendment to the Constitution of the United States.

_____

_____

2. Section 1101(1) of title 11 of the current *United States Code*, published in 2006. This section appears in its entirety in the 2006 main volume.

_____

_____

3. Subsection (a)(6) of section 523 of title 11 of the current *United States Code*, published in 2006.

_____

_____

4. Section 15(b)(1) of title 15 of the current *United States Code*, published in 2006.

_____

_____

5. Section 547(c)(3) of title 11 of the current *United States Code*, published in 2006.

_____

_____

6. Rule 43(b) of the current Federal Rules of Civil Procedure, published in the Appendix to title 28 of the *United States Code* in the 2005 Supplement V.

_____

_____

7. Rule 804(a) of the current Federal Rules of Evidence, published in the Appendix to title 28 of the *United States Code* in the 2005 Supplement V.

_____

_____

8. Section 231v(a) through (c) of title 45 of the current *United States Code*. These subsections appear in their entirety in the 2005 Supplement V.

_____

_____

9. In a discussion of the current version of certain federal tax law provisions, cite section 2036(a) of the Internal Revenue Code, title 26 of the current *United States Code*, published in 2006. Use the special citation form for tax law provisions.

_____

_____

10. Section 1332(a)(2) of title 28 of the current *United States Code*, all of which was printed in the main volume published in 2006.

_____

_____

Chapter 7

STATE STATUTES

Rule 14.4 generally governs state statute citations. The rule, however, basically serves to refer you to each state's listing in Appendix 1. Please read Rule 14.4 and glance through your state's listing in Appendix 1.

The citation form for federal statutes and state statutes is similar; however, the challenge here is that each state has a different system of compiling and publishing statutes. Thus, each state has a slightly different citation form for statutes. Generally, each citation will include the following:

- an abbreviated name of the state code;
- possibly the name of a subject matter if the code is arranged by subject matter;
- numerical information pointing the reader to a specific statutory provision;
- possibly the publisher of the code; and
- the year of publication.

In each state's entry in Appendix 1, you will find a template for what information to include and in what form. This listing also includes the proper abbreviation for each state code. Therefore, for each state statute that you cite, you should always refer to that state's page in Appendix 1 for a fool-proof "formula." You may also need to consult Rule 2.2 to ensure that you are spacing the abbreviation correctly.

Most statutes are not organized by pages as cases are. Instead, most statutes are arranged by sections, but may also be arranged by chapters, titles, paragraphs, subdivisions, or a combination thereof. Therefore, in addition to consulting Appendix 1, you will also need to pay attention to Rule 6.1 with regard to sections and paragraphs. Broadly, remember that you indicate that you are citing to multiple sections by using two section symbols without a space in between. Note, however, that you need a space between the section symbol and the actual section number.

Ariz. Rev. Stat. §§ 17-454, 17-456 (Lexis 2006).

Del. Code Ann. tit. 3, § 10105(a) (Lexis 2001).

Alaska Stat. § 37.14.400 (Lexis 2006).

The only other detail you need to know to master the basics of state statute citation is how to determine the date of the code. Note that the year of the code is NOT the date the particular statute was enacted. To avoid this confusion, remember the purpose of the date in the citation: to help your reader know how to find a particular statute. To do this, your reader must know what version of a code to consult, *i.e.*, the version of the code published in a particular year. In addition, your reader must know whether the information is contained in the main body of the code, a supplement or pocket part, or both. Therefore, you need to include this information. Rule 8.2 tells us to glean the date of the code for date parenthetical purposes from the date on the copyright page. If the entirety of the section that you are citing appears in the main volume, use only the date for the main volume.

> Del. Code Ann. tit. 7, § 931 (Lexis 2001).

Often, part or all of the section will have been amended and reprinted in a supplementary volume that is either bound separately from the main volume or attached in a pocket located in the inside back cover of the main volume. Rule 8.3 gives insight into citing material that appears in both the main volume and the supplement.

> Del. Code Ann. tit. 7, § 927 (Lexis 2001 & Supp. 2006).

Many times, a newly enacted statute will appear only in the supplement or pocket part. In these cases, you should include only the year of the supplement pursuant to Rule 8.1.

> Del. Code Ann. tit. 7, § 517(c) (Lexis Supp. 2006).

Lastly, some states, such as California and Michigan, have more than one statutory compilation. Generally, the *ALWD Manual* prefers citations to the official state code, if possible. Appendix 1 indicates which compilation to cite, if available, by noting each official code with a star (☆).

Checklist for State Statutes

- Have you consulted Appendix 1 for the correct abbreviation of the state code?
- Have you followed the format for the state statute given in Appendix 1?
- Have you taken the year of the code from the copyright information in the appropriate volume?
- Does all of the information cited appear in the main volume?

  - If so, then include only the year of the main volume in the parenthetical.
  - If a portion of the statute cited is in a supplement, then include the date of the main volume and the supplement.

- Does all of the information cited appear in a supplement? If so, then include the date of only the supplement.

Exercise 7

State Statutes

Put the following information in correct *ALWD* citation form. All statutes are being cited in citation sentences. Although this exercise builds on the rules used in previous exercises and generally follows Rule 14.2 for federal statutes, this exercise focuses on state rather than federal statutes. You will need to refer to Rules 13 and 14.4 and Appendix 1 for information on the statutes in the appropriate jurisdiction.

1. Section 291-52 of Michie's *Hawaii Revised Statutes*, all of which appears in the 2007 pocket part.

_____

_____

2. Sections 213.10887 and 213.1099 of Michie's *Nevada Revised Statutes Annotated*, parts of which appear in both the 2005 main volume and the 2007 cumulative supplement.

_____

_____

3. Section 16-6-2(a) of the official version of the *Official Code of Georgia Annotated*. The copyright date is 2007. No amendments to this section appear in any supplement or pocket part.

_____

_____

4. Section 18.2-387 of the *Code of Virginia Annotated*. The copyright date is 2004. No amendments to this section appear in any supplement or pocket part.

_____

_____

5. Section 41.181(4)(a) of the *Michigan Compiled Laws Annotated*. This section appears in its entirety in the 2006 main volume.

_____

_____

6. Section 45-2-102(A) of Michie's *Annotated Statutes of New Mexico*. The title page of the volume that contains this section states the date of publication as 2004.

_____

_____

7. Section 31-231 of the *Arizona Revised Statutes*, which is found only in the 2002 main volume.

_____

_____

8. Section 1632(a) through (c) of West's *Annotated California Civil Code*. The copyright date on the volume in which this statute appears is 1985. Certain amended paragraphs also appear in the 2008 cumulative pocket part.

_____

_____

9. Section 60K of chapter 231 of the *Massachusetts General Laws Annotated*, published by West. The copyright date on the volume in which this statute appears is 2000, but the entire section is amended and reprinted in the 2008 pocket part.

_____

_____

10. Section 24-3-205 of the *Arkansas Code Annotated*. This section appears in its entirety in the 2000 main volume.

_____

_____

11. Section 35.01 of the *Arts & Cultural Affairs Laws of New York Annotated*, which is published in a volume of McKinney's *Consolidated Laws of New York Annotated*. This entire section appears in the 2008 pocket part.

_____

_____

12. Title 17, section 2512 of the *Maine Revised Statutes Annotated*. The entire relevant section appears in the 2007 pocket part.

_____

_____

13. Title 54, section 355(D) of the *Oklahoma Statutes*. The copyright date of this volume is 2000. This section does not appear in any supplement or pocket part.

_____

_____

14. Title 6, section 18-108 of the *Delaware Code Annotated*. The copyright date is 2005. This section does not appear in any supplement or pocket part.

15. Subsections 36-4-2(1) through (4) of the *General Laws of Rhode Island*. These sections appear in their entirety in the 2006 pocket part.

Chapter 8

SHORT FORMS (STATUTES)

As with cases, you will often refer to a statute several times within a legal memorandum or a court document. Similarly, the *ALWD Manual* states that you need to give the full legal citation for a statute only the *first* time that you cite to that statute. Thereafter, you will use a short form citation to that statute. Rule 14.6 and Rule 11 provide information on short form citations for state and federal statutes. Rule 13.4 gives us guidance as to short form citations for state and federal constitutions. You should read each of those sections carefully before attempting Exercise 8.

As with cases, the *ALWD Manual* provides two types of short forms to be used for statutes in legal memoranda and court documents: "*id.*" and an abbreviated version of the full legal citation. The rules for when you may use each type parallel the rules that we discussed in connection with cases. You may use the short form "*id.*" only when you are citing to a statute previously cited in the immediately preceding citation (and only if that previous citation is not a string cite). Again, no intervening cites to a different authority of any type should appear between the previous cite to this statute and the current citation.

You learned in Exercise 5 (Short Forms (Cases)) that you use "*id.*" to refer to a previous case even when you want to cite to a different page. Similarly, the previous citation to a statute need not be to the exact section or subsection of your statute; however, you will need to include any information in your citation that differs from the immediately preceding citation. As you did in case short forms, use the word "at" in a statutory short form when referring to a different section or subsection of a statute. The proper formulation is simply the word "*id.*" followed by "at" and the new section or subsection information.

Because Rule 11.3(b) tells you that you should indicate in an "*id.*" cite only the way in which that citation differs from the previous one, you will omit the code abbreviation and the date and publisher parenthetical, provided that the material is the same for the "*id.*" cite as for the original citation. However, you should reproduce the entire section number for clarity if only the subsection changes. Although this rule is not stated expressly, it can be inferred from the examples following Rule 14.6. Notice in the example below that the second citation includes both the section and subsection information rather than just the different subsection. Notice that the third citation includes also the date parenthetical because section 1–201(b)(2) is in the 2003 Supplement, but the original section cited was in the 1997 main volume.

> In our jurisdiction, "fruit" is defined as an edible part of a plant that contains seeds. **St. Stat. Ann. § 1-201(a) (1997).** A "vegetable" is defined as an edible part of a plant that does not contain seeds. ***Id.* at § 1-201(b)(1).** However, the term "vegetable" does not include legumes

or tubers. *Id.* Recently, the legislature determined that a cucumber, although it contains seeds, would be deemed to be a vegetable. *Id.* **at § 1-201(b)(4) (Supp. 2003).**

In those circumstances when you wish to use a short form but cannot use "*id.*," you will use an abbreviated form of the full citation. Rule 14.6 gives you several abbreviation options. You may omit just the date parenthetical, omit the title of the publication and the date parenthetical, or omit the title of the publication, any chapter or title number, and the date parenthetical. This concept is easier to convey in examples:

36 U.S.C. § 301 (2006).

becomes:

36 U.S.C. § 301.

or

§ 301.

Md. Code Ann. Fin. Inst. § 13–708.1 (2003).

becomes:

Md. Code Ann. Fin. Inst. § 13–708.1.

or

§ 13-708.1

Vt. Stat. Ann. tit. 13 § 2405 (2002).

becomes:

Vt. Stat. Ann. tit. 13 § 2405

or

tit. 13 § 2405.

or

§ 2405.

You will eventually develop your own preferences, but your ultimate objective should be clarity for your reader.

Checklist for Statutory Short Forms

- Did you cite to the current statute in the immediately preceding citation? If not, then you cannot use "*id.*"
- Does the immediately preceding citation contain more than one authority, *i.e.*, is it a string cite? If so, then you cannot use "*id.*"
- If you cannot use "*id.*," have you formulated an acceptable abbreviated short form?
- Have you remembered to include the word "at" in your short form?

Exercise 8

Short Forms (Statutes)

Put the following information in correct *ALWD* citation form. All statutes are being cited in citation sentences. Although this exercise builds on the rules used in previous exercises, this exercise focuses on Rules 11.2–11.4, 13.4, and 14.6. You will need to refer to Appendix 1 for information on the statutes in the appropriate jurisdiction.

1. In the immediately preceding sentence of a legal memorandum, you cited to a provision in the *California Civil Code*, Cal. Civ. Code Ann. § 1559 (West 1982). Without an intervening cite, you wish to cite to this same statute.

\
\

2. On the next page of your memorandum, after citing to several other authorities, you wish to cite to Cal. Civ. Code Ann. § 1559 (West 1982). In your memo, you have cited to statutes from other states and to provisions in other California subject matter codes. You are concerned that your reader may be confused, so you want your short form to be clear.

\
\

3. In the very next sentence of your memorandum, without an intervening cite, you wish to cite to another provision of the *California Civil Code*, Cal. Civ. Code Ann. § 1556 (West 1982).

\
\

4. Earlier in the same general discussion, you cited to Idaho Code § 29-102 (1996). Now, two pages later, you wish to cite to section 29-101. Several cites to other authorities appear on the two intervening pages. You have not cited to any other statutes in this memo and think the shortest abbreviation will be best because there is no risk of confusion to the reader.

\
\

5. On page 3 of a different memorandum, you cited to a provision of the *Code of Virginia Annotated*, Va. Code Ann. § 8.2-716(1) (2001). In the next line, you again cite to the same provision, using the short form *"id."* In the next paragraph, without any intervening cites, you wish to cite to subsection (2) of the same provision.

\
\

6. In the same paragraph, without any intervening cites, you again wish to cite to subsection (2) of Va. Code Ann. § 8.2-716.

_____

_____

7. In an appellate brief, you wish to cite to section 5342(b) of the *California Corporations Code*. The immediately preceding cite reads "Cal. Corp. Code Ann. § 5342(b) (West 1990); Cal. Civ. Code Ann. § 1559 (West 1982)." Because you are citing to several California codes, you are concerned with the risk of confusion to your reader.

_____

_____

8. In a legal memorandum, you have previously cited to a New York statute, N.Y. Crim. Proc. Law § 700.05(1)–(2) (McKinney 1995). Three paragraphs later, with several intervening cites to different authorities, you wish to cite to the same two subsections. Because you are citing to several New York subject matter codes, you are concerned that your reader will be confused unless you identify each statute with particularity.

_____

_____

9. In the next sentence, without any intervening cites, you wish to cite to subsection (8)(a) of section 700.05. However, this subsection has been amended in its entirety and appears only in the 2008 pocket part.

_____

_____

10. In a legal memorandum, you have previously cited to a portion of the Maine state constitution, Me. Const. art. I, § 3. After several intervening cites to other authorities, you wish to cite to the same provision.

_____

_____

Chapter 9

COMPREHENSIVE CORE EXERCISE

After completing the first eight exercises, you are well on your way to mastering legal citation! Let's stop, catch our breath, and review what you have learned.

By now, you should know how to cite any case decided by a court in the United States, whether state or federal. Also, if you are citing a case to a state court and that state requires parallel citation to a state reporter and a regional reporter, you know how to construct that parallel citation. You also know how to use "*id.*" and how to formulate short forms for case citations.

Similarly, you know how to cite to any statute, state or federal. You are also comfortable using "*id.*" and short forms to refer to statutes that you have already referenced in a full citation.

With these skills, you can cite to most authoritative sources and produce a professional legal memorandum or court document. In the next exercises, we are going to introduce you to the concept of citation signals, which "signal" to your reader the importance of citations if the connection between the source and your proposition is not clear in the text alone. You will also learn how to add explanatory parentheticals to your citations to reinforce and clarify the importance of those citations. We will also explore other types of sources, such as books, treatises, law review articles, and legislative resources.

Before we continue marching on, you may want to try Exercise 9: Comprehensive Core Exercise, which will reinforce the skills learned in Exercises 1–8. To help you get back into the swing of things, the following is a list of common mistakes first-year law students make in basic citation:

- Forgetting to put a court designation in the court and date parenthetical when the reporter information is not sufficient.
- Guessing on the abbreviations in case names instead of checking Appendix 3.
- Omitting the volume and reporter information in a case short form: *i.e.*, "Casper, 99 U.S. at 310," **not** "Casper, at 310."
- Omitting the comma between the case name and the volume information in a case short form.
- Omitting the space between "F." and "Supp." and "2d" for cases reported in *Federal Supplement* ("F. Supp." and "F. Supp. 2d").
- Omitting a date parenthetical in a full citation of a statute.

Finally, remember your successful completion of these exercises does not mean that you should never consult the *ALWD Manual* again. Most student citation mistakes arise when students think they remember what the *ALWD Manual* says, but do not actually look up the rule. The best legal writers are not those that memorize the *ALWD Manual*, but those who know when to open it.

Exercise 9

Comprehensive Core Exercise

Put the following information in correct *ALWD* citation form. Assume that the authority is being cited in citation sentences in a brief to the United States Supreme Court unless otherwise noted. For pinpoint citations, use a hyphen for page spans and repeat *all* digits on both sides of the span. This exercise reviews the skills you learned in Exercises 1 through 8.

1. Lawrence A. Schmid, Plaintiff, versus Robert A. Frosch, Administrator of NASA, Defendant. This case was decided in the United States District Court for the District of Columbia on January 30, 1985. It appears in volume 609, page 490, of *Federal Supplement* and in volume 36, page 1687, of *Fair Employment Practice Cases*.

2. On page 23 of your brief and in the same section of the discussion, you gave a full cite to the case in #1. On page 26 of your brief, you would like to refer to this case again, focusing your reader's attention on information beginning on page 495 of the opinion and continuing on page 496. You have cited to other cases in the interim. The case name does not appear in the textual sentence.

3. Section 26640 of West's *Annotated California Government Code*. The date on the copyright page is 2008 and no amendments appear in the pocket part or supplement.

4. You wish to cite again to section 26640 of West's *Annotated California Government Code* in the next paragraph of your brief. You have cited to two cases since your last reference to section 26640. This is the only statute in your brief, so you would prefer to keep your short form as short as possible.

5. In a brief submitted to the Supreme Court of Texas, you wish to cite to W.R. Grace & Company versus Maryland Casualty Company, et al. This case was decided in the Appeals Court of Massachusetts on September 30, 1992. It appears in volume 33, page 358, of *Massachusetts Appeals Court Reports* and in volume 600, page 176, of *North Eastern Reporter*, Second Series.

6. Section 3129(a) of title 7 of the *United States Code*, published in the 2006 main volume.

_____

_____

7. Section 8, clause 8 of Article I of the Constitution of the United States.

_____

_____

8. One paragraph later, after citing to a federal statute, you wish to cite again to section 8, clause 8 of Article I of the Constitution of the United States.

_____

_____

9. Ernest E. Jones, Terrence A. Larsen, and Herbert Lotman versus Raymond W. Smith and Peter S. Strawbridge. This case was decided by the Supreme Court of Pennsylvania on January 6, 1999. It appears in volume 734, page 862, of *Atlantic Reporter*, Second Series. The citation follows a direct quotation of material found on page 865 of the opinion.

_____

_____

10. Paula Corbin Jones, Plaintiff, versus William Jefferson Clinton and Danny Ferguson, Defendants. This case was decided by the United States District Court for the Eastern District of Arkansas, Western Division, on July 29, 1999. It appears in volume 57, page 719, of *Federal Supplement*, Second Series.

_____

_____

11. In your brief, you cited to the case in #10 in the immediately preceding sentence. In the next sentence, without any intervening cites, you would like to cite to that case again. However, this time you would like to direct your reader's attention to information found on page 723.

_____

_____

12. Federal Rule of Civil Procedure rule 20(a), dealing with permissive joinder of parties, published in the appendix to title 28 of the *United States Code* in the 2005 Supplement V.

_____

_____

13. Section 4711 of title 16 of the *Delaware Code Annotated*. The date 2003 appears on the copyright page.

14. In a brief submitted to the Supreme Court of Virginia, you wish to cite to the State of Georgia versus Ronnie Jack Beasley, Jr. This case was decided by the Supreme Court of Georgia on July 30, 1998. It is reported in volume 269, page 620 of *Georgia Reports* and in volume 502, page 235, of *South Eastern Reporter*, Second Series.

15. In a brief to the Supreme Court of Georgia, you have previously cited to the case in #14, using a parallel citation form. You wish to cite to this case again on the next page of your brief after several intervening cites, focusing your reader on information contained on page 623 of the state reporter and 239 of the regional reporter. The case name is not mentioned in the textual sentence.

16. Section 498.033(1)–(7) of the *Florida Statutes Annotated*, published in 2006 by West.

17. In the next sentence, you wish to cite to just subsection (3) of the Florida statute. You have not included any intervening citations.

18. Oliver Brown, et al., versus The Board of Education of Topeka, Kansas. This case was decided by the United States Supreme Court on May 17, 1954. It appears in volume 347, page 483, of *United States Reports*; in volume 74, page 686, of *Supreme Court Reporter*; and in volume 98, page 873, of *Lawyers' Edition*, Second Series.

19. On page 68 of your brief, you cite to the case in #18. On page 72 of your brief and in the same section of the brief after citing to other authorities, you would like to refer to this case again, focusing your reader's attention on information on page 485 of U.S., page 688 of S. Ct., and page 875 of L. Ed. 2d. You have been referring to this case throughout your brief as *Brown*. The case name is not mentioned in the textual sentence.

---

20. Federal Rule of Evidence 609(a)(i) published in the appendix to title 28 of the *United States Code* in the 2005 Supplement V.

Chapter 10

PRIOR & SUBSEQUENT CASE HISTORY

Now that you have mastered a basic case citation, you are ready to add a more advanced skill: prior and subsequent history. You probably have learned by now that one case may go through several levels of appeal in its life. At each level, the court reviewing the case may publish an opinion. Opinions issued by courts that review the case after the opinion you wish to cite are called *subsequent history*. Opinions issued by courts before the opinion you wish to cite are called *prior history*. As you read through this chapter, you may find helpful the examples in Rules 12.8, 12.9, and 12.10. These rules tend to be pretty detailed and complex, but remember: you need not memorize any citation rules. You only need to understand how they work and where to find them so you can refresh your understanding.

To illustrate this, let's use the fictional case of *Bait v. Switch*. *Bait v. Switch* started out as a negligence lawsuit in federal trial court in the Northern District of Texas. Bait was awarded damages by the trial court, and the trial court issued an opinion. This opinion was reported in *Federal Supplement*. Switch then appealed to the Fifth Circuit Court of Appeals. The Fifth Circuit affirmed the trial court's judgment and also issued an opinion, which was published in *Federal Reporter*, Third Series. Finally, Switch filed a writ of certiorari to the United States Supreme Court. The United States Supreme Court denied certiorari, issuing an opinion explaining the reason for the denial. This opinion was reported in several reporters, including *United States Reports*. So we have three different courts that have dealt with this case and issued opinions. The Fifth Circuit Court of Appeals and United States Supreme Court opinions are *subsequent history* to the federal trial court opinion.

N.D. Tex.	5th Cir.	U.S.

subsequent history

The federal trial court and Fifth Circuit opinions are *prior history* to the United States Supreme Court opinion.

N.D. Tex.	5th Cir.	U.S.

prior history

The Fifth Circuit opinion has both prior and subsequent history — the federal district court opinion is prior history, and the United States Supreme Court opinion is subsequent history.

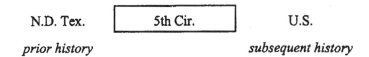

N.D. Tex.   5th Cir.   U.S.

prior history   **subsequent history**

You will find citations to prior and subsequent history by using a citator service such as *Shepard's*. You should receive instruction on how to use a citator in your legal research class.

Rule 12.8 governs subsequent history. Rule 12.9 governs prior history. Rules that apply to both subsequent and prior history are found in Rule 12.10. The general rule for subsequent history is that any action listed in Rule 12.8(a) should be included when you cite an opinion in full. (This means that short cites should not include prior or subsequent history.) However, this rule has exceptions.

Include subsequent history unless . . .

- **the history is a denial or dismissal of certiorari or appeal and the cited case (not the denial or dismissal) is more than two years old** *but:* include denials of cert. or appeal if they are particularly important to your discussion (see Sidebar 12.6 for guidance on what is "particularly important"), or
- **the history is history on remand, rehearing, or rehearing en banc.**
- **the history is a denial or dismissal of certiorari or appeal and the cited case (not the denial or dismissal) is more than two years old** *but:* include denials of cert. or appeal if they are particularly important to your discussion (see Sidebar 12.6 for guidance on what is "particularly important"), or
- **the history is history on remand, rehearing, or rehearing en banc.**

The general rule for prior history is that it should be used sparingly and should be cited only when it is important for the point you are discussing.

When would prior history be important to a discussion? Let's go back to *Bait v. Switch*. Assume we want to cite the Fifth Circuit's opinion in *Bait v. Switch* because it is favorable to the point we are arguing. However, the Fifth Circuit opinion does not include as full a description of the facts in that case as the district court opinion does. If we wanted to analogize our facts closely to those of *Bait v. Switch* to argue that our client's case should be decided the same way the Fifth Circuit decided *Bait*, we might give the prior history of *Bait v. Switch* (the federal district court opinion) so we could use the lower court's description of the facts.

So now that you know **when** to give prior and subsequent history, you're ready to learn **how** to do it. Rules 12.8(c) and 12.9(b) tell us that the prior or subsequent history will follow the full citation of the primary case. This usually means that the history cite will follow the court and date parenthetical. However, if the primary case cite includes an additional parenthetical (for explanation, weight of authority, etc. — all things you will cover in Chapter 12), then the history cite follows that parenthetical.

A history cite must be introduced by an explanatory phrase. The explanatory phrases for subsequent history are listed in Rule 12.8(a). This rule also shows how the phrases should be italicized and punctuated. Notice that the comma following the phrase *should not* be italicized. The explanatory phrases for prior history are formed by converting the phrases in Rule 12.8(a) from "*-ed*" verbs to "*-ing*" verbs (*e.g.*, "affirmed" becomes "affirming"). Although a comma follows phrases introducing subsequent history, no comma follows phrases introducing prior history. These explanatory phrases give the reader important information about the relationship between the cases cited. For example, what if we want to cite *Bait v. Switch* (the district court opinion) for Proposition A, but it has been reversed in *Switch v. Bait* (the Fifth Circuit opinion) for the lower court's error on Proposition B? Although *Bait v. Switch* is no longer good law for Proposition B, it is still good law for Proposition A. To let your reader know that you are aware of the reversal but that it has no impact on your argument, you would introduce your subsequent history cite with the explanatory phrase "*rev'd in part on other grounds.*"

Sometimes, a case requires several history citations. If you give both a prior and a subsequent history citation, Rule 12.10(c)(2) requires that the prior history be listed first and followed with the italicized word "*and*" and followed by the subsequent history.

Most of the subsequent history you will note will be in the cited case's direct line. For example, all of the opinions in the *Bait v. Switch* example involve the same parties and the same litigation. However, Rule 12.8(a)(14) tells you to note as subsequent history cases that overrule a cited case, regardless of whether the cases are otherwise related.

What happens if the case name changes on appeal? Rule 12.10(b) covers this. If the names are simply reversed on appeal, then you do nothing. Cite the case name as it appears in the primary case you are citing and simply give a citation without a case name for the prior or subsequent history. The same is true if the history cite is a denial of certiorari.

But what if the first-named party changes on either or both sides? Not all parties that are involved in one phase of a case are necessarily involved in subsequent appeals. If you want to indicate a different name for a prior or subsequent history, add the phrase "*sub nom.*" to your explanatory phrase and give the case name along with its citation. When using "*sub nom.*" following an explanatory phrase, omit the comma that would ordinarily follow the phrase.

That's a lot of explanation, but the drafting is really not bad. Let's try an example. Because we are familiar with Bait and Switch, let's use their case and assume that we have the following citations to work with:

trial court:	*Bait v. Switch*, 111 F. Supp. 222 (N.D. Tex. 1994).
intermediate court of appeals:	*Switch v. Bait*, 333 F.3d 444 (5th Cir. 1994).
court of last resort:	*Switch v. Jones*, 555 U.S. 666 (1995).
unrelated case:	*Duck v. Cover*, 777 U.S. 888 (1997).

First, let's assume that we want to cite the intermediate court of appeals opinion in the Bait and Switch litigation. So, we start with that citation:

> *Switch v. Bait*, 333 F.3d 444 (5th Cir. 1994).

We start with the general rule that we include subsequent history. So we consider whether to include the citation to *Switch v. Jones*. If *Switch v. Jones* was simply a denial of certiorari by the United States Supreme Court, we would not include it. Why? The decision in *Switch v. Bait* is older than two years. Therefore, the denial of certiorari would not be included. However, *Switch v. Jones* is not just a denial of cert.; let's say that when we look up *Switch v. Jones*, we discover that the Supreme Court heard the case and issued an opinion affirming the Fifth Circuit's decision in *Switch v. Bait*. However, it affirmed the Fifth Circuit on different grounds from those for which we intend to cite the case. First, we will need to turn to Rule 12.8(a) to find out what explanatory phrase to use. Turning to Rule 12.8(a)(2), we see *"aff'd on other grounds,"* — that looks like exactly what we need. Notice that we will replace the period at the end of the original citation sentence with a comma and save the period for the new end of our citation sentence.

> *Switch v. Bait*, 333 F.3d 444 (5th Cir. 1994), *aff'd on other grounds,*

Notice that a comma follows the phrase, and remember that the comma *should not* be italicized.

Now it's time for the history citation. To name or not to name. Well, the party names are not simply reversed (*Switch v. Bait* and *Switch v. Jones*), and this is not a denial of certiorari. Rather, we have a subsequent history citation with a different name. So follow Rule 12.10(b) and add *"sub nom."* to the explanatory phrase and then give the case name along with the other citation information. Notice that no comma follows *"sub nom."*

> *Switch v. Bait*, 333 F.3d 444 (5th Cir. 1994), *aff'd on other grounds sub nom. Switch v. Jones*, 555 U.S. 666 (1995).

Let's try it the other way around: cite *Switch v. Jones* with *Switch v. Bait* as prior history. The exact same explanatory phrase that we used for subsequent history will not work for prior history. Remember that Rule 12.9(b)(2) tells us that we convert the phrase by changing the verb ending from *"-ed"* to *"-ing."* So we'll change *"aff'd on other grounds"* to *"aff'g on other grounds."*

> *Switch v. Jones*, 555 U.S. 666 (1995), *aff'g on other grounds sub nom. Switch v. Bait*, 333 F.3d 444 (5th Cir. 1994).

Now, let's cite *Bait v. Switch* with all its subsequent history. Remember that Rule 12.10(c) says we can just attach the additional history to the citation. Let's assume that each court affirmed the court below it:

Bait v. Switch, 111 F. Supp. 222 (N.D. Tex. 1994), *aff'd*, 333 F.3d 444 (5th Cir. 1994), *aff'd sub nom. Switch v. Jones*, 555 U.S. 666 (1995).

Notice that we do not include a case name for the Fifth Circuit's opinion because the name is just a reversal of the cite before it (the primary cite of *Bait v. Switch*). However, we do include the case name for *Switch v. Jones* because it names different parties than the lower court opinions.

Okay, one more twist on Messrs. Bait and Switch. Let's cite the Fifth Circuit opinion, giving both prior and subsequent history. Remember that Rule 12.10(c)(2) tells us to include prior history first and to join the subsequent history with the word "*and.*" Again, assume that the case was affirmed all the way up.

Switch v. Bait, 333 F.3d 444 (5th Cir. 1994), *aff'g* 111 F. Supp. 222 (N.D. Tex. 1994), *and aff'd sub nom. Switch v. Jones*, 555 U.S. 666 (1995).

See? You're getting the hang of it! Let's assume that Bait, Switch, and Jones never went to the Supreme Court. They only got as far as the Fifth Circuit before they got tired of the whole thing. However, a few years later a similar case did go to the Supreme Court, and the Supreme Court's opinion in that case (*Duck v. Cover*) overruled what the Fifth Circuit had to say in *Switch v. Bait*. That would be important history to note any time you cite *Switch v. Bait*. You would do that according to Rule 12.8(a)(14):

Switch v. Bait, 333 F.3d 444 (5th Cir. 1994), *overruled, Duck v. Cover*, 777 U.S. 888 (1997).

Okay, now you're ready to make history on your own! Because these rules are so detailed, you may find the following checklists especially helpful in completing the exercise.

Checklist for Subsequent Case History

- Is there any reason not to include subsequent history?

    - The answer is yes if the subsequent history citation is . . .

        - an irrelevant denial of certiorari or other appeal on a decision older than two years, or
        - a history on remand, rehearing, or rehearing en banc.
    - Otherwise, continue . . .
- Have you replaced the period at the end of the primary citation with a comma (remember that the history cite follows the *entire* primary cite, even if the primary cite includes explanatory or other types of parentheticals)?
- Have you introduced your citation with an italicized explanatory phrase?
- Have you italicized the explanatory phrase but not the comma that follows it?
- Do you need to include the case name in the history cite?

    - The answer is no if . . .

        - the party names are simply reversed, or
        - the history cite is a denial of certiorari.
    - Otherwise, include the case name.
- If you included a case name, have you added "*sub nom.*" to your explanatory phrase and deleted any comma following the phrase?
- If you included prior history in the citation as well, did you place the prior history first and join the subsequent history with "*and*"?
- If you have multiple subsequent history dispositions, have you listed them consecutively without the word "*and*" to join them?
- Did you end your full citation sentence with a period?

Checklist for Prior Case History

- Do you need prior history at all?

    - Is the earlier case significant to the point the primary case is being cited for?
- Have you replaced the period at the end of the primary citation with a comma?
- Have you introduced your citation with an italicized explanatory phrase converted from the subsequent history phrases in Rule 12.8(a)?
- Do you need to include the case name in the history cite?

    - The answer is no if . . .

        - the party names are simply reversed, or
        - the history cite is a denial of certiorari.
    - Otherwise, include the case name.
- If you included a case name, have you added "*sub nom.*" to your explanatory phrase?
- If you included subsequent history in the citation as well, did you place the prior history first and join the subsequent history with "*and*"?
- If you have both prior and subsequent histories, have you joined them with "*and*"?

- If you have multiple prior histories, have you listed them consecutively without the word "*and*" to join them?
- Did you end your full citation sentence with a period?

Exercise 10

Prior & Subsequent Case History

Put the following information in correct *ALWD* citation form. All cases are being cited in citation sentences in a brief to the United States Supreme Court. Although this exercise builds on the rules used in previous exercises, this exercise focuses on Rules 12.8, 12.9 and 12.10. Unless the problem states otherwise, you should assume that case names are the same at each level of appeal. Remember that you must decide *whether* to include a history cite before you decide *how* to include one. The first case listed in each problem is the case you need to cite.

1. You want to cite Benitec Australia, Limited v. Nucleonics, Incorporated. This case is an October 20, 2007, federal case from the Federal Circuit Court of Appeals. It is reported in volume 495, page 1340, of *Federal Reporter*, Third Series. The United States Supreme Court denied certiorari in April 2008. That denial is not yet reported in *United States Reports* but is reported in volume 128, page 2055 of *Supreme Court Reporter*. You cite the case in a brief filed on October 3, 2009. The denial of certiorari has no impact on the argument you are drafting.

_____

_____

_____

2. You want to cite Brad Bennett, et al., versus Marvin L. Plenert, in his official capacity as Regional Director, Region One, Fish and Wildlife Service, U.S. Department of the Interior, et al. This is a 1995 federal case from the Fifth Circuit Court of Appeals published in volume 63, page 915, of *Federal Reporter*, Third Series. This case deals with both First Amendment and Due Process issues. You are citing the case in support of a First Amendment issue. However, the case was reversed in part in 1997 on Due Process grounds. The reversal is published in volume 520, page 154, of *United States Reports*.

_____

_____

_____

3. James Flanagan, et al., versus Gerald Ahearn, et al. This is a 1996 federal case from the Fifth Circuit Court of Appeals published in volume 90, page 963, of *Federal Reporter*, Third Series. The United States Supreme Court vacated this decision in an opinion published as *Ahearn v. Flanagan*, 521 U.S. 1114 (1996).

_____

_____

_____

4.   Janice E. Hetzel versus County of Prince William. This is a 1996 federal
     case from the Fourth Circuit Court of Appeals published in volume 89,
     page 169, of *Federal Reporter*, Third Series. The petitioner requested
     that the United States Supreme Court hear the case on an issue
     unrelated to the issue for which you are citing the case. The Supreme
     Court denied certiorari in 1996 in a decision published in volume 519,
     page 1028, of *United States Reports*.

_____

_____

_____

5.   You want to cite the case of Milton Knapp, Petitioner, versus Mitchell D.
     Schweitzer, Judge of the Court of General Sessions. This 1958 United
     States Supreme Court Case is published in volume 357, page 371, of
     United States Reports; in volume 78, page 1302, of *Supreme Court
     Reporter*; and in volume 2, page 1393, of *Lawyers' Edition*, Second
     Series. This case was overruled in 1964 by the case of William Murphy
     and John Moody, Sr., Petitioners, versus The Waterfront Commission of
     New York Harbor. That case is published in volume 378, page 52, of
     United States Reports; in volume 84, page 1594, of *Supreme Court
     Reporter*; and in volume 12, page 678, of *Lawyers' Edition*, Second
     Series.

_____

_____

_____

6.   Edward Silva, Jr., versus The United States of America. This 1995
     federal case from the Ninth Circuit Court of Appeals is published in
     volume 51, page 203, of *Federal Reporter*, Third Series. The United
     States Supreme Court first dismissed certiorari of this case in 1995. This
     dismissal is published in volume 515, page 1189, of *United States Reports*.
     The Supreme Court subsequently denied certiorari in 1995. The denial is
     published in volume 516, page 973, of *United States Reports*. Both the
     dismissal and the denial were on issues for which you intend to cite the
     Court of Appeals opinion and are, therefore, particularly important to the
     discussion.

_____

_____

_____

7. Haitian Centers Council, Inc., Plaintiffs-Appellants, versus Gene McNary, Commissioner, Immigration and Naturalization Services, Defendants-Appellants. This 1992 federal case from the Second Circuit Court of Appeals is reported in volume 969, page 1350, of *Federal Reporter*, Second Series. The United States Supreme Court reversed this decision as Chris Sales, Acting Commissioner, Immigration and Naturalization Service, et al., Petitioners, versus Haitian Centers Council, Inc., et al. This 1993 case is reported in volume 509, page 155, of *United States Reports*.

---

8. You wish to cite Benjamin Lee Lilly, Petitioner, versus the Commonwealth of Virginia. This 1999 United States Supreme Court case is reported in volume 527, page 116, of *United States Reports*. This decision reverses the decision of the Supreme Court of Virginia in this case. The Virginia Supreme Court's 1998 opinion explains the issues more clearly and thoroughly and is published in volume 225, page 522, of *South Eastern Reporter*, Second Series.

---

9. Charles Carlisle, Petitioner, versus The United States of America. This 1996 United States Supreme Court case is reported in volume 517, page 416, of *United States Reports*. This decision affirms the 1995 decision of the Sixth Circuit Court of Appeals in this case. That 1995 opinion, which explains the issues more clearly and thoroughly, is published in volume 48, page 190, of *Federal Reporter*, Third Series.

---

10. United States of America versus Stacey C. Koon. This 1994 federal case from the Ninth Circuit Court of Appeals is reported in volume 34, page 1416, of *Federal Reporter*, Third Series. The Ninth Circuit reversed the 1993 trial court decision from the Central District of California, located at volume 833, page 769, of *Federal Supplement*, which gives the best explanation of the issues in this case. The Ninth Circuit was later reversed by the United States Supreme Court in a 1996 decision reported in volume 518, page 81, of *United States Reports*.

Chapter 11

SECONDARY SOURCES

By now, you are highly proficient in citing any type of case law or legislative enactment. But you may want to cite to information located in other sources such as books, law reviews, and periodicals. You may even find yourself needing to cite to something more esoteric like a letter or a telephone interview. The *ALWD Manual* dedicates many rules, beginning with Rule 22, to citing secondary sources such as these in their original media. Because you are already proficient in citing sources of positive law, citing these other print sources will be a snap.

However, you may be doing more and more of this type of research over the Internet or through an electronic database. Chapter 15 will explore how to cite sources found through these types of research. This chapter will focus on citing the original print source. Please review the rules mentioned below before attempting Exercise 11.

A. Books

Rule 22 governs generally the citation of "books" — nonperiodic monographs. The basic citation form for a book will contain information regarding:

- the full name of the author or authors,
- the title of the book,
- the editor and/or translator, if any,
- the publisher, and
- the date.

If you would like to send your reader to a specific page or pages in the book, the page number would immediately follow the title.

Author, *Title* Pg. (Editor, Publisher Date).

Rule 22.1(a) tells you to give the author's name just as it appears. Unlike other citation systems you may have learned in your undergraduate or graduate studies, you do not rewrite the name to put the surname first. If the book has two authors, include both names joined by an ampersand (&) in the order that the names appear in the book.

Jonathan Harr, *A Civil Action* (Vintage 1997).

Burton Silver & Heather Busch, *Dancing with Cats* (Chron. Books 1999).

If the book has several authors, include all names as a series, with the names separated by commas and the last two names connected by an ampersand. Alternatively, if the work has three or more authors, Rule 22.1(a)(2)(d) gives us the option of using the phrase "et al." after the first name.

J. Myron Jacobstein, Roy Mersky & Donald J. Dunn, *Fundamentals of Legal Research* 121 (7th ed., Foundation Press 1998).

or:

J. Myron Jacobstein et al., *Fundamentals of Legal Research* 121 (7th ed., Foundation Press 1998).

The next piece of information that your reader will need after the author is the title of the work. You should include the full title as it appears on the title page. Do not alter the title by abbreviating or omitting words, but capitalize according to Rule 3, which tells you to capitalize all words except articles, conjunctions, and prepositions. Rule 3 also tells us to always capitalize the first word in a title or subtitle and the first word following a colon.

Paul Alexander, *Salinger: A Biography* (Renaissance Books 1999).

Remember, the overriding concern in legal citation is that the reader should have enough information to find the exact source that you are citing. Therefore you will need to include the editor or translator, Rule 22.1(d) and (e), even if the book has an author. The name of an editor will be followed immediately by the abbreviation "ed." and the name of a translator will be followed immediately by the abbreviation "trans." If a book has two editors or translators, then both names will appear and be followed immediately by "eds." or "trans." respectively. If a book has an editor and a translator, then the editor's name and designation appear first, followed by a comma and the translator information. Editor and translator information appears in the date parenthetical.

Gabriel Garcia Marquez, *Love in the Time of Cholera* 69–70 (Edith Grossman trans., Knopf 1988).

Sometimes, a book will not have a specific author, only an editor. In this situation, no author information will appear, and the editor information will appear in the date parenthetical.

The Antarctic Treaty Regime (Gillian D. Triggs ed., Cambridge U. Press 1987).

Another piece of information that must appear in the date parenthetical is the publisher information. Rule 22.1(i) tells us to always include the name of the publisher, abbreviated according to Appendix 3 and Appendix 5, after any editor or translator information, but before the year of publication.

The last piece of information you must include is the date of publication. Many books have only one publication date. However, some books are published in several editions. If you are citing to an edition other than the first edition, Rule 22.1(f) tells you to include the edition number (after any editor or translator information but before the publisher information). This information is necessary for your reader to be able to consult a source that you are citing by page number. The page numbers of various editions will not be consistent, so your reader will need to know exactly what edition you are citing. Good legal writers cite to the latest edition, unless context requires otherwise.

> J. Myron Jacobstein, et al., *Fundamentals of Legal Research* 121 (7th ed., Foundation Press 1998).

One last rule. If you are citing to a modern version of a work published before 1900, Rule 22.1(j)(6) gives you the option of including the original date of publication in a separate parenthetical at the end of your citation. For example, if you are citing a work of literature, you would include in the date parenthetical the name of the publisher and the date of the edition that you are citing. You would also include the original publication date in a separate parenthetical.

> Thomas Hardy, *Tess of the D'Urbervilles* (David Skelton ed., Penguin Books 1978) (originally published 1891).

B. Collections

Many books that you will cite will be collections of articles or essays. These sources follow the rule for shorter works in collection, Rule 22.1(m). In your legal citation, you must include:

- the full name of the author of the specific work that you are citing,
- the title of the specific work,
- the author of the collection, if any,
- the title of the collection,
- the page number on which the specific work begins,
- the editor and translator, if any,
- the publisher, and
- the date.

Author, *Work Title*, in *Collection Title* Pg. (Editor, Publisher Date).

The name of the author will appear in ordinary roman type, and the titles of both the specific work and the collection will appear in italics.

> Anthony A. Peacock, *Strange Brew: Tocqueville, Rights, and the Technology of Equality*, in *Rethinking the Constitution: Perspectives on Canadian Constitutional Reform, Interpretation, and Theory* 122, 125–156 (Anthony A. Peacock ed., Oxford U. Press 1996).

In addition, some frequently cited books have special citation forms. For example, Rule 22.1(n) gives you the citation forms for *The Bible*.

C. Periodicals

You will also on occasion cite to articles in periodicals and law reviews. Rule 23 provides rules on citing to all periodical materials. The basic form is similar to the form used for shorter works in a collection. In your legal citation, you must include

- the full name of the author of the article that you are citing,
- the title of the article,
- the volume of the periodical, if any,
- the title of the publication and any other pertinent volume or series information,
- the page number on which the specific work begins, and

- the date.

First, the author information will appear in your citation exactly like the author information in a book citation. Then, the title of the article will appear in italics. Next, you will include the volume number of the periodical, if any. Law reviews are organized by volumes, which generally correspond to an academic year. However, each "volume" may be printed in separately bound publications with edition numbers. For example, Volume 22 of a certain law review may actually span three separately bound publications, which are usually soft-bound editions. Each publication may be given a number: Volume 22, No. 2. Once a volume is complete, the soft-bound numbered editions are collected and permanently bound as one volume. Therefore, the pages in each publication are numbered beginning with page 1 in Volume 22, No. 1 and ending with the last page of Volume 22, No. 3. Because of this numbering system, only the volume number and the page number are necessary to point your reader to the correct publication.

Stephen R. Heifetz, *Blue in the Face: The Bluebook, the Bar Exam, and the Paradox of Our Legal Culture*, 51 Rutgers L. Rev. 695 (1999).

However, if your periodical does not have a volume number, like magazines and newspapers, then you omit this step entirely.

The next piece of information in your citation will be the abbreviation of your periodical title. Appendix 5 lists abbreviations for most legal periodicals. If the name of the periodical does not appear in Appendix 5, you can fashion your own by abbreviating all words listed in Appendix 3. Many times, the name of your nonlegal periodical will have no abbreviation at all.

Samantha Miller & Dan Jewel, *Brat Race*, People 114 (April 19, 1999).

If your periodical is a newspaper, then you may want to include a parenthetical immediately after the periodical name with the place of publication. If the place of publication is well-known, then this step is not necessary.

Edmund L. Andrews, *Total Fina Is Victorious with Bid for Elf Acquitaine*, N.Y. Times, C1 (Sept. 14, 1999).

After your periodical abbreviation, simply insert the page on which the article begins. The final piece of information, as you may have guessed, is a date parenthetical. Rule 23.1(f)(2) tells us to include only the year of publication if our periodical is consecutively numbered throughout a certain volume or year, like a law review. If the periodical is not consecutively paginated, then you will need a more specific date. Include the most exact date listed, abbreviating months according to Appendix 3.

Nadine Strossen, *The Fourth Amendment in the Balance: Accurately Setting the Scales through the Least Instrusive Alternative Analysis*, 63 N.Y.U. L. Rev. 1173 (1988).

Steven Pinker, *Horton Heard a Who?*, Time 86 (Nov. 1, 1999).

On very rare occasions you will need to cite to a source that is unpublished in a written medium. Rule 31 covers interviews; Rule 32, letters; Rule 36, forthcoming works; and Rule 37, unpublished works, including working papers compiled on public databases.

Exercise 11

Secondary Sources

Put the following information in correct *ALWD* citation form. All sources are being cited in citation sentences. This exercise focuses on Rules 22 through 37. You should follow the convention of placing one space after a colon, period, or question mark within a title.

1. "Can a Good Christian Be a Good Lawyer? Homilies, Witnesses, & Reflections," a book published in 1998 by the University of Notre Dame Press, Thomas A. Baker and Timothy W. Floyd, editors.

   _____

   _____

   _____

2. "The Brethren," a book by Bob Woodward and Scott Armstrong, published by Simon & Schuster in 1979, pages 196–208.

   _____

   _____

   _____

3. "In a Different Voice," a book by Carol Gilligan, published in 1982 by the Harvard University Press.

   _____

   _____

   _____

4. "Crime and Punishment," a book by Fyodor Dostoevsky, originally published by a different publisher in 1865, translated by Constance Garnett and published in 1927 by Grosset & Dunlap.

   _____

   _____

   _____

5. An article by Bill Piatt entitled "The Confusing State of Minority Language Rights," included in a compilation of articles entitled "Language Loyalties: A Sourcebook on the Official English Controversy," published in 1992 by the University of Chicago Press and edited by James Crawford. The article begins on page 229.

   _____

   _____

   _____

6. An article entitled "Milberg Weiss: Of Studied Indifference and Dying of Shame" found on page 209 in volume 2 of the Journal of Business & Technology Law, published in 2007. The author of the article is Theresa A. Gabaldon. Remember, most law journals are consecutively paginated.

_____

_____

_____

7. An article entitled "Women & HIV: A Gender-Based Analysis of a Disease and Its Legal Regulation" by Mary Anne Bobinski, found on page 7 of volume 3 of the Texas Journal of Women and the Law, published in 1994. You wish to focus the reader's attention on pages 14–15 of that article. Remember, most law journals are consecutively paginated.

_____

_____

_____

8. An article in the April 1999 issue of Smart Money magazine entitled "Confessions of a Fund Manager" by Landon Thomas Jr. The article begins on page 104.

_____

_____

_____

9. An article appearing on page 2, section B, in the October 4, 2008 edition of the New York Times entitled "Google and Yahoo Delay Ad Deal for Antitrust Review." The author of the article is Miguel Helft.

_____

_____

_____

10. Introduction beginning on page ix by M.S. Handler to the Ballantine Books 1965 edition of the book "The Autobiography of Malcolm X," written by Alex Haley.

_____

_____

_____

11.   An article in the December 16, 1999 issue of "Newsweek" magazine entitled "The World According to Google," by Steven Levy. The article begins on page 46.

_____

_____

_____

12.   An article entitled "Punitive Damages and Business Organizations: A Pathetic Fallacy," by John J. Kircher, found on page 971 of volume 6 of the Tennessee Law Review, published in 2000.

_____

_____

_____

Chapter 12

PARENTHETICALS

We know that legal citation serves two primary purposes: to give attribution to a source and to give locating information for a source. In addition, you have probably learned in your legal writing course that citations can also help make your writing more concise. Your citation can minimize or eliminate the need for some detailed explanation. For example, citations can give the year of decision and the jurisdiction of the case so that you do not have to give that information textually.

Instead of:

In 1995, the Texas Supreme Court held that false imprisonment is the willful detention of another without that person's consent and without authority of law. *Randall's Food Mkts., Inc. v. Johnson*, 891 S.W.2d 640 (Tex. 1995).

You can write:

False imprisonment is the willful detention of another without that person's consent and without authority of law. *Randall's Food Mkts., Inc. v. Johnson*, 891 S.W.2d 640 (Tex. 1995).

Citation parentheticals and signals provide additional citation tools for giving your reader useful information without including that information in a detailed discussion. In this chapter, you will learn how to use parentheticals. In the next chapter, you will learn how to use parentheticals with signals.

You have probably noticed in your legal reading that a great deal of information of several kinds is enclosed in parentheses at the end of some citations. This information falls generally into two categories: weight of authority and explanation. Weight of authority parentheticals give the reader information that indicates the precedential value of a cited case.

Welsh v. U.S., 398 U.S. 333 (1970) **(plurality).**[1]

Explanatory parentheticals provide additional information to make clear to the reader the reason for the citation.

In re Marriage of Wood, 567 N.W.2d 680 (Iowa App. 1997) **(upholding an order modifying child support and requiring the father to contribute toward college expenses of the children).**

While weight of authority parentheticals are only used with case citations, explanatory parentheticals may be used with any type of authority cited.

---

[1] Information appears in bold print in this book for highlighting purposes only. You should not format any part of your citations in bold print.

A. Weight of Authority Parentheticals

Rules 12.11(a) and 12.11(b) explain how the case's precedential value should be included in a citation. Generally, two types of information indicate that the case does not have the same value as other cases decided by the same court — information that indicates the weight of the authority (*e.g.*, en banc, per curiam, 5–4 decision, dictum) and information that shows that the proposition cited is not the clear holding of the majority of the court (*e.g.*, dissenting, concurring, or plurality opinions). For example, dictum of the Supreme Court does not have the same value as a holding of the majority of the Court. Therefore, the fact that you are citing dictum of the Supreme Court is necessary to your reader's understanding of the value of your cited authority. You can indicate parenthetically that the information you have cited is dictum:

(dictum)

Similarly, a quotation of text from a dissenting opinion would not have the same weight as a quotation from the majority opinion. In that case, the parenthetical would look like this:

(O'Connor, J., dissenting)

In drafting weight of authority parentheticals, be guided by the examples in Rules 12.11(a) and 12.11(b).

B. Explanatory Parentheticals

Legal writers sometimes include information in explanatory parentheticals to citations to provide additional information that makes clear to the reader the relevance of the citation. Parentheticals provide a clear, concise, economical means of getting the maximum information to the reader with a minimum of detailed explanation. Their use is especially helpful when the writer does not really want to discuss the parenthetical information in text but still considers it necessary to help the reader fit the citation into the overall picture.

Rule 12.11(c) suggests using explanatory parentheticals with cases, and Rule 14.2(b) suggests using them with statutes. However, parentheticals can be used with any type of cited authority. Rule 46 gives the general rules for including explanatory parentheticals in citations to any source. The following discussion is applicable to all types of authority.

Most often, explanatory phrases begin with the present participle form of a verb (one that ends in *-ing*).

W. Wendell Hall, *Standards of Review in Texas*, 29 St. Mary's L.J. 351, 354 (1998) (**explaining** the difference between the standards of review for "no evidence" and "insufficient evidence").

Because the explanation is a phrase, it does not need a period within the parentheses. If the context of the citation makes a participle phrase unnecessary, a shorter phrase may be used:

The interviewer may be anyone authorized to investigate employment matters. *See e.g. Black v. Kroger Co.*, 527 S.W.2d 794 (Tex. Civ. App. —

Houston [14th Dist.] 1975, no writ) (**store manager**); *Safeway Stores, Inc. v. Amburn*, 388 S.W.2d 443 (Tex. Civ. App. — Fort Worth 1965, no writ) (**security guard employed by Safeway**).

In addition to explaining the relevance of a cited authority, parentheticals can also be used to explain the relationship between two sources:

La. Stat. Ann. §§ 2317, 2322 (1979) (**codifying** the rule in *Coulter v. Texaco, Inc.*, 547 F.2d 909, 913 (5th Cir. 1977)).

Meeker v. Hamilton Grain Elevator Co., 442 N.E.2d 922, 927 (Ill. 1982) (**quoting** *Bonebrake v. Cox*, 499 F.2d 951, 953 (8th Cir. 1974)).

C. Order of Parentheticals

Because case citations may include both weight of authority parentheticals and explanatory parentheticals, legal writers need a rule to guide them in ordering multiple parentheticals. Rule 46.2(b) requires that parentheticals that must be included as part of the citation appear before explanatory parentheticals. Because weight of authority parentheticals must accompany a citation, they should always be placed before explanatory parentheticals.

O'Connor v. Bd. of Educ., 449 U.S. 1301, 1306 (1980) (**Stevens, J., concurring**) (**affirming an order vacating a temporary injunction**).

If the citation also includes prior or subsequent history, Rule 47.2(a) requires that the parenthetical follow the source to which it relates.

Bennett v. Plenert, 63 F.3d 915 (5th Cir. 1995) (**holding that ranchers and irrigation districts were not within zone of interests protected by ESA**), *rev'd in part on other grounds*, 520 U.S. 154 (1997).

Mastery of the art of drafting explanatory parenthetical phrases will help you become a polished, professional legal writer — one who gets his or her point across in the fewest possible words. With a few well-chosen words in a parenthetical phrase, you will be able to communicate the crux of a case or other authority without discussing it at all in text.

D. Dry Run

Let's walk through the process of figuring out (1) whether a citation needs a parenthetical and (2) if it does, how to put it together.

Suppose we want to cite *Smith v. Brown*, 123 U.S. 456, 467 (1970). We are citing Justice Euclid's concurring opinion. Concurrences do not have the same precedential value as majority opinions. Accordingly, Rule 12.11(a) indicates that we need a parenthetical phrase because the proposition for which the case is cited is not the majority opinion. The examples following 12.11(a) show that we should convey the appropriate weight of authority by adding the following parenthetical after the basic citation:

(Euclid, J., concurring).

Although this is a well-known case, we wish to cite it for one of its lesser-known propositions. Therefore, an explanatory parenthetical is also needed to make the citation's relevance clear.

So we must decide what to say and how to say it in the parenthetical. We are citing page 467 of the case on which Justice Euclid says in dictum that if X were Y, the jury's verdict would not have been allowed to stand. In our brief, we are arguing that the general rule represented by *Smith v. Brown* should not apply to our client's case because, on our facts, X *is* probably Y. How can we word that in an explanatory parenthetical so that it will be clear and concise?

First, the parenthetical phrase should probably begin with a present participle verb. We cannot use "holding" because the statement was dictum and appeared in a concurring opinion. Instead, we could use "suggesting" for our first word. For the rest, we can simply say "that if X were Y, the jury's verdict would not have been allowed to stand." Although we could quote the court's language in our parenthetical, the better practice is to paraphrase unless the actual words of the court are particularly memorable or concise.

Finally we must decide in what order to put the parenthetical phrases. Rule 47.2(b) guides us here. The weight of authority parenthetical must precede the explanatory parenthetical. So the completed citation would look like this:

Smith v. Brown, 123 U.S. 456, 467 (1970) (Euclid, J., concurring) (suggesting that if X were Y, the jury's verdict would not have been allowed to stand).

Notice the one space between each set of parentheses and the period at the end of the citation sentence *outside* the closing parenthesis.

Checklist for Parentheticals

- Have you checked each applicable rule (Rules 12.11, 14.2(h), and 46) to be sure you are including all the parentheticals you need?
- If the case has less precedential value than the court's clear majority opinions, have you included a weight of authority parenthetical that follows the examples in Rule 12.11(a) and (b)?
- If the relevance of the cited authority is not clear, have you included an explanatory parenthetical that follows the examples in Rule 46?
- If you have both weight of authority and explanatory parentheticals, have you placed the weight of authority parenthetical first?
- If your citation includes prior or subsequent history, have you placed the parenthetical(s) immediately after the court and date parenthetical of the cited authority as shown in Rule 46.2(a)?
- Have you left only one space before the parenthetical?
- Have you put the period ending your citation sentence *outside* the closing parenthesis?

Exercise 12

Parentheticals

Put the following information in correct *ALWD* citation form. All sources are being cited in citation sentences. Assume that all citations will appear in a brief to a federal court. Although this exercise builds on the rules used in previous exercises, this exercise focuses on Rules 12.11, 14.2(h), and 46. Remember that each case name must be italicized according to Rule 12.2(a).

Note: In these problems, the wording for any explanatory phrase will appear in the text of the problem in quotation marks. Changes in wording will be read online as an error. This should not be construed as meaning that explanations have one "right" phrasing. This is simply a limitation imposed by the ICW's software.

1. Elliott Ashton Welsh, II, versus United States, a 1970 United States Supreme Court plurality decision (*i.e.*, a case in which there was no majority opinion) reported in volume 398, page 333, of *United States Reports*.

---

2. A consolidated 1989 United States Supreme Court case, County of Allegheny, et al., versus the American Civil Liberties Union, Greater Pittsburgh Chapter, et al., and Chabad versus the American Civil Liberties Union, et al., City of Pittsburgh versus American Civil Liberties Union Greater Pittsburgh Chapter, reported in volume 492, page 573, of *United States Reports*. You want to refer specifically to material appearing on page 601 in the concurring opinion of Justice Sandra Day O'Connor. [*Hint: The American Civil Liberties Union is commonly referred to by its initials.*]

---

3. Geraldine Coulter, wife of James Coulter, and James Coulter, Plaintiffs-Appellants, versus Texaco, Inc., Texas Exploration and Production, Inc., and Rogers Louviere, Defendants-Appellees, an opinion of the Fifth Circuit Court of Appeals reported in 1997 in volume 117, page 909, of *Federal Reporter*, Third Series. You want to draw attention particularly to material on page 913 of the opinion "citing articles 2317 and 2322 of the Louisiana Civil Code Annotated, published by West in 1979." [*Note: You must properly draft the citation for articles 2317 and 2322 to include in your parenthetical.*]

---

4. Triad Electric & Controls, Inc., Plaintiff/Counter-Defendant Appellant/ Cross-Appellee, versus Power Systems Engineering, Inc., et al., Defendants/Counter-Plaintiffs Appellees/Cross-Appellants, a 1997 opinion of the Fifth Circuit Court of Appeals published in volume 117, page 180, of *Federal Reporter*, Third Series. You want to quote material on page 192. You want to indicate in your citation that the court in *Triad* quoted the same material from a case titled T.J. Stevenson & Company, Inc., versus 81,193 Bags of Flour, etc., a 1980 Fifth Circuit Court of Appeals case published in volume 629, page 338, of *Federal Reporter*, Second Series. The quotation was taken from pages 369 and 370 of *T.J. Stevenson*.

---

5. You wish to cite section 777.011 of *Florida Statutes Annotated*, published by West, for its statement "establishing that presence is not required for responsibility as a principal in the first degree." This section appears entirely in the 2000 main volume.

---

6. Robert Michael Lawyer, Appellant, versus Linda Lorraine Lawyer, Appellee. This is a 1986 opinion of the Arkansas Supreme Court reported in volume 288, page 128, of *Arkansas Reports*, and in volume 702, page 790, of *South Western Reporter*, Second Series. You want to cite the dissenting opinion of Justice Hays, specifically the portion "stating that the legislative purpose behind § 34-1214 should not be frustrated." This statement appears on page 133 of *Arkansas Reports* and on page 793 of *South Western Reporter*, Second series. [*Note: Remember that your brief is to be filed in federal court.*]

---

7. In a brief to the United States Supreme Court, you wish to cite Henry F. Hartlove, Personal Representative of the Estate of Claude Faye Bass, versus the Maryland School for the Blind, a 1996 opinion of the Maryland Court of Special Appeals reported in volume 111, page 310, of *Maryland Appellate Reports*, and in volume 681, page 584, of *Atlantic Reporter*, Second Series. You want to cite this case specifically for its "holding that a litigant may not use a jury instruction as a vehicle for adding a cause of action" on page 315 of *Maryland Appellate Reports* and on page 687 of *Atlantic Reporter*, Second Series.

_____

_____

_____

8. You wish to cite Lucent Information Management, Incorporated versus Lucent Technologies, Incorporated. This is a 1997 federal case from the district court for the District of Delaware. It is reported in volume 986, page 253, of *Federal Supplement*. Although you do not plan to elaborate on this case in text, you want the reader to know that its significance is its "holding that trademark ownership is acquired by adoption and use according to common law traditions." The Third Circuit Court of Appeals affirmed the district court's holding in 1998 in an opinion reported in volume 186, page 311, of *Federal Reporter*, Third Series.

_____

_____

_____

9. United States, Plaintiff-Appellee, versus John Javilo McCullah, Defendant-Appellant, a 1996 opinion of the Tenth Circuit Court of Appeals published in volume 76, page 1087, of *Federal Reporter*, Third Series. You want the reader to know that the significance of this case is the court's "remanding the case to the trial court for re-sentencing."

_____

_____

_____

10. "The Ethical Obligations of Prosecutors in Cases Involving Post-conviction Claims of Innocence," an article by Judith A. Goldberg and David M. Siegel of California Western School of Law. The article was published in Spring 2002 in volume 38 of the consecutively-paginated California Western Law Review. This article "outlining the significance of standards for reviewing issues arising under innocence-based post-conviction review statutes" begins on page 389. [*Note: The word "post-conviction" contains a hyphen even when printed on a single line.*]

_____

_____

_____

Chapter 13

SIGNALS

In the previous chapter, you learned that you can add parenthetical explanations to give your reader helpful information without making that information part of the text of your document. Citation signals are another tool you can use to give valuable information without a detailed explanation. Before reading the rest of this chapter, read Rules 44.2 and 44.3 so you will be familiar with the type and identity of the signals available to you. Reading through the explanations of the signals first will provide a context for the following discussion.

You have probably noticed citation signals in citations in the legal reading you have done already. Signals can properly be used with any kind of cited authority. The purpose of signals is to show the reader how the authority cited relates to what the text says and, in some cases, how it relates to other material in the same citation sentence. When you use a signal to describe the relationship between text and citation, Rule 44.4 strongly encourages a parenthetical explanation to elaborate on that relationship.[1]

Because the primary purpose of signals is to give the reader information without a detailed textual discussion, writers often take full advantage of signals by using one signal to introduce more than one source. If you intend for the same signal to apply to all sources cited in a citation sentence, the signal should not be repeated with each source — rather the signal will be presumed to apply to all sources following it (see example below). When signals introduce more than one source, the sources are separated by semi-colons and ordered according to Rule 45.4, Order of Cited Authorities. Rule 45.4 tells us how to order different types of authority in a single citation sentence (*e.g.*, cases and statutes) and also how to order authority of only one type in a single citation sentence (*e.g.*, cases from several jurisdictions). For example, if a citation sentence includes both a case and a journal article, Rule 45.4 instructs that the case (Rule 45.4(a)(4)) should be listed before the article (Rule 45.4(c)(3)).

> *Contra City of Los Angeles v. Lyons*, **461 U.S. 95** (1983); Brandon Garrett, Student Author, *Standing While Black: Distinguishing Lyons in Racial Profiling Cases*, **100 Colum. L. Rev. 1815** (2000).

On the other hand, if a citation sentence includes only cases, Rule 45.4(a)(4) gives the order of cases within the sentences and Rule 45.3(h) says that cases decided by the same court should be listed in reverse chronological order.

---

[1] So you can more easily locate and focus on the signals used in this chapter's examples, the examples do not include parenthetical explanations.

See e.g. Heath v. Jones, 817 S.W.2d 335 (**Tex. 1991**); *Cooper v. Smith*, 527 S.W.2d 898 (**Tex. 1975**); *Ludwick v. Miller*, 931 S.W.2d 752 (**Tex. App. — Fort Worth 1996**, no writ).

Writers can also maximize the use of signals by using more than one signal in a citation sentence. This is helpful when you want to describe both the relationship of the citations to the text and the relationship of the citations to one another. When using different signals in a single citation sentence, signals should appear in the order listed in Rule 44.3. In addition, Rule 44.8(c) requires that the different signals be separated by a semi-colon and a single space.

> ***See*** *State v. Michaels*, 642 A.2d 1372 (N.J. 1994); ***but cf.*** *Commonwealth v. Allen*, 665 N.E.2d 105 (Mass. App. 1996).

As with all other parts of a legal citation, signals have specific typeface rules. Introductory signals in citations are always italicized as provided in Rules 1.3(a) and 44.6(b). Remember, too, that a citation sentence has the same capitalization rules as a textual sentence: The first word must be capitalized. Therefore, a signal that begins a citation sentence is capitalized; otherwise, the signal is not capitalized.

> ***See*** *State v. Michaels*, 642 A.2d 1372 (N.J. 1994); ***but cf.*** *Commonwealth v. Allen*, 665 N.E.2d 105 (Mass. App. 1996).

Before you begin the exercise, let's go through an example of a citation that uses a signal and a parenthetical.

Suppose we write that "if a person is a farmer, then he is not a rancher." Although we don't have a source that directly says that, it is implied in the holding of *Rancher v. Farmer*, 888 P.2d 222 (Mont. 1985), that "farmers engage exclusively in one vocation." The question is, how can we indicate that without having actually to discuss the case in text? Easy: Introductory signals to the rescue!

First, look at Rule 44.0, the signal rule. Quickly scanning 44.3, we see that the signal "see" seems to fit our situation because it signals that the cited authority implicitly supports the textual proposition.

> *See Rancher v. Farmer*, 888 P.2d 222 (Mont. 1985)

We remember from Rule 44.4 that we should use an explanatory parenthetical anytime we use a signal. Parentheticals usually begin with an "*-ing*" verb that describes what the source does or says, so the first thing we want to do is choose a verb to begin our parenthetical. Because we are relying on what the court held in *Rancher v. Farmer*, we can begin the parenthetical with "holding" and then state the holding of the court:

> (holding that farmers engage exclusively in one vocation)

Remember that the explanatory parenthetical follows the completed citation, so our entire citation, complete with parenthetical, will look like this:

> *See Rancher v. Farmer*, 888 P.2d 222 (Mont. 1985) (holding that farmers engage exclusively in one vocation).

Remember to put a single space between the court and date parenthetical and the explanatory parenthetical. Also remember that the period at the end of the citation sentence goes outside the closing parenthesis.

There's one thing to be careful of when using the signal of *"compare . . . with."* Although the rules and examples do not specifically address this, no punctuation should follow the first citation's last parenthetical.

> *Compare Rancher v. Farmer*, 888 P.2d 222 (Mont. 1985) (holding that farmers engage exclusively in one vocation) *with Driver v. Walker*, 222 A.2d 444 (N.J. 1945) (holding that one cannot walk and drive simultaneously).

And that's all there is to it!

Checklist for Signals

- Does your authority directly state the proposition, identify the source of a quotation, or identify an authority you mentioned in text?

  - If so, you can skip the rest of this checklist because Rule 44.2(a) tells us that no signal is required.
  - If not, you must have a signal, so continue.

- Have you selected the appropriate signal from Rule 44.3?
- Have you italicized the signal?
- Have you capitalized the signal if it is the first word of your citation sentence?
- Have you drafted an explanatory parenthetical to explain the relevance of your citation? (A quick review of the Chapter 12 checklist may be helpful.)
- Have you put the period that ends the citation sentence outside the final closing parenthesis?

Exercise 13

Signals

Put the following information in correct *ALWD* citation form. All sources are being cited in citation sentences. Although this exercise builds on the rules used in the previous exercises, this exercise focuses on Rules 44.0 and 45.0. Determine what, if any, introductory signal you should use and what, if any, parenthetical explanation you should include.

Note: Although some citations lend themselves to alternative signal choices, be guided by the wording in the problem in choosing a signal. When the correct answer includes a signal, it will also include an explanatory parenthetical. As in the Parentheticals exercise, the wording for any needed parenthetical phrase will appear in quotation marks in the problem.

1. You write that "a father's failure to attend counseling mandated by court order is a sufficient change in circumstances to modify an earlier visitation order." Although your research did not find a case directly on point for this proposition, you did find a case "holding that a father's failure to use alternative dispute resolution procedures mandated in a prior court order constituted a change in circumstances sufficient to modify a support order." This case is Peter Q. Harris versus Bonnie L. Harris. This is a 1998 opinion of the Supreme Court of Vermont reported in volume 714, page 626, of *Atlantic Reporter*, Second Series. The holding in *Harris* supports your proposition only by analogy. Draft the citation that should follow your statement.

    _____

    _____

    _____

2. In a brief to the United States District Court for the District of Kansas, you write that "a natural parent's right to custody is a fundamental right guaranteed by the Fourteenth Amendment." This proposition is supported implicitly by many opinions in which courts have rejected claims by non-natural parents on the basis that those parents' rights were not guaranteed by the Fourteenth Amendment. However, a citation to one of those opinions will be sufficient to make your point. You have chosen a Supreme Court of Kansas case to illustrate the point. That opinion is In the Matter of the Guardianship of Nolynn Glendon Williams, a minor child. This is a 1994 case "holding that absent extraordinary circumstances, the parental preference doctrine is to be applied." This case is reported in volume 254, page 814, of *Kansas Reports*, and in volume 869, page 661, of *Pacific Reporter*, Second Series. Draft the citation that should follow your statement. [*Note: Remember that the brief will be filed in a federal district court.*]

    _____

    _____

    _____

3. In a brief to an Alabama trial court, you quote directly from the case of Lisa Michelle Phillips versus Jack Lawrence Phillips. This is a court of Civil Appeals of Alabama case decided on October 31, 1997, and reported in volume 705, page 512, of *Southern Reporter*, Second Series. Your quotation is taken from the dissenting opinion of Justice Crawley on page 513. Draft the citation that should follow your quotation.

    _____

    _____

    _____

4. In a brief to the Hawaii Supreme Court, you write that "insurance contracts covering property within the State of Hawaii may not contain provisions depriving Hawaii courts of jurisdiction over those contracts." This rule comes directly from section 43:10-221 of the *Hawaii Revised Statutes* main volume published in 2000. Draft the citation that should follow your statement.

    _____

    _____

    _____

5. In a motion to dismiss filed in federal district court for the District of Connecticut, you write that "states disagree about whether grandparent visitation statutes may be invoked only in the course of other custody proceedings." You wish to offer support for this proposition by comparing two cases from courts that reached opposite conclusions. The first case is *Frame v. Nehls* "holding that the state's grandparent visitation statute did not apply in a paternity action because it was not an action for child custody." *Frame* is a 1996 Michigan Supreme Court case reported in volume 550, page 739, of *North Western Reporter*, Second Series. The second case is Castagno, et al. versus Wholean, et al., "reversing the dismissal of a grandparent's visitation petition for lack of jurisdiction in the absence of death, divorce, or a child custody proceeding." *Castagno* is a 1996 Supreme Court of Connecticut case reported in volume 684, page 1181, of *Atlantic Reporter*, Second Series. Draft the citation that should follow your statement. [*Note: Remember to order authorities using Rule 45.4.*]

    _____

    _____

    _____

6. In an office memorandum to your supervising attorney, you write that "grandparent visitation statutes are gaining popularity." To provide authority as helpful background information for this statement, you want to cite a 1995 law review note (as distinguished from a law review article) in volume 29, page 835, of the consecutively-paginated *Suffolk University Law Review*. The title is "Court-Ordered Families: An Overview of Grandparent Visitation Statutes." The note "providing a survey of grandparent visitation statutes from all states that have enacted them" was written by Michael Quintal. Draft the citation that should follow your statement.

_____

_____

_____

7. In a brief to the Supreme Court of Wyoming, you write that "a state statute providing a five-year limitation period for paternity actions is constitutionally valid under the Equal Protection clause." In the interest of fairness, you wish to direct the court's attention to a concurring opinion in a 1996 Supreme Court of Wyoming case, State of Washington ex rel. DAA v. CJH. This case is reported in volume 923, page 758, of *Pacific Reporter*, Second Series. The concurring opinion, by Justice Macy, "stating that, if properly brought before the court, the court would rule that a limitation period on paternity actions is unconstitutional because it discriminates between illegitimate and legitimate children" appears on page 763. This statement directly contradicts the position you have advocated in text. Draft the citation that should follow your statement.

_____

_____

_____

8. In a brief to the Utah Supreme Court, you have quoted and discussed at length a case from the New York Supreme Court, Appellate Division, which raises the issue you are analyzing with facts that are virtually identical to your client's situation. To make the persuasive value of this case clear to the Utah Supreme Court, you wish to indicate at the conclusion of that paragraph that the law of the State of Utah is consistent with the New York law discussed. For this, you have chosen a 1997 Utah Supreme Court case "holding that, for the purpose of determining the validity of a trust, the interest of any beneficiary other than the grantor suffices." The case is In the matter of the Estate of Sharon W. Groesbeck versus David J. Groesbeck, and is reported in volume 935, page 1255, of *Pacific Reporter*, Second Series. Draft the Utah citation that should follow your discussion of the New York case.

_____

_____

_____

9. In a brief to the Supreme Court of Nebraska, you write that "alimony is exempt from some limitations on garnishments." You inferred this statement from an opinion of the Supreme Court of Nebraska "holding that alimony was exempt from the 15% cap on garnishment of the ex-husband's Social Security benefits." This holding was articulated in Mary Jo Kropf, Appellee, versus Frederick J. Kropf, Appellant. This is a 1995 Supreme Court of Nebraska case reported in volume 248, page 614, of *Nebraska Reports*, and in volume 538, page 496, of *North Western Reporter*, Second Series. Draft the citation that should follow your statement.

    _____

    _____

    _____

10. In a brief to a Nebraska trial court, you wish to cite *Hopkins v. Batt*. This is a 1998 Supreme Court of Nebraska case reported in volume 253, page 852, of *Nebraska Reports*, and in volume 573, page 425, of *North Western Reporter*, Second Series. You wish to indicate in your citation that this court reached the same holding as the case you have been discussing in text. Although *Hopkins* is distinguishable in some respects from the case you have been discussing, it supports the proposition you have just stated in text by its "citing section 42-377 of the *Revised Statutes of Nebraska* (published in the 1993 main volume)." Draft the citation that should follow the proposition in text. [*Note: You must properly draft the citation for section 42-377 to include in your parenthetical.*]

    _____

    _____

    _____

Chapter 14

LEGISLATIVE RESOURCES

Legislative history and administrative resources can be seen as the bookends bracketing volumes of statutes. Legislative history documents reflect and give insight into the process by which a particular bill either becomes or does not become enacted law. At the other end of the process, the regulatory agencies promulgate regulations that put the enacted statute into effect. The documents generated by regulatory agencies and by the rest of the executive branch of government are collectively referred to as administrative resources. Accordingly, rules governing use and citation of legislative resources begin in Chapter 15, following Chapter 14, which covers enacted statutes. Chapter 19 contains provisions for citing administrative and executive resources. For convenience, this chapter of the ICW is divided into two subsections: legislative history resources and administrative resources.

A. Legislative History

This chapter and the accompanying exercises focus exclusively on federal materials. States vary widely in the publication of legislative materials, but many state legislative materials are patterned generally after the federal model. Therefore, the citation of legislative history follows the same general principles, whether federal or state. The citation of state legislative materials is governed by a separate chapter, Chapter 16, which is not analyzed here.

In an increasingly codified legal system, statutory interpretation becomes a vital skill in many areas of legal practice. Often, a legal writer will rely on the intent of the legislature enacting a statute to properly interpret that statute. Legal writers look to the documents that are produced in the legislative process to determine that legislative intent.

To understand how to cite these documents, let's refamiliarize ourselves with the path a proposed law takes through Congress on its way to becoming "law." A proposed law may be presented in either house as a bill, a resolution, a joint resolution, or a concurrent resolution. For unenacted legislation, citation of these four types is essentially the same. Let's trace a wholly fictional bill from a Congressman's desk into the pages of the *United States Code*.

In the first session of the 104th Congress, Representative Blue introduces a bill he calls the Excellence in Legal Writing Act of 1996. This bill is the 911th bill introduced into the House of Representatives during this session, so the number given to the bill is H.R. 911. If our bill had been a resolution, the number abbreviation would be "H.R. Res. 911." Rule 15.1(a) lists abbreviations for all types of proposed laws.

H.R. 911, 104th Cong. (May 1, 1996).

Rule 15.1(g) tells us that we may include the title of the bill or resolution. If you decide to include the title, place it at the beginning of your citation in ordinary type.

Excellence in Legal Writing Act, H.R. 911, 104th Cong. (May 1, 1996).

Our bill is referred to the House Committee on Education, which in turn refers it to its subcommittee on Improvement of the Legal Profession, which then conducts hearings. The printed transcript of the hearing held September 11, 1996, shows on its cover the title "Excellence in Legal Writing Act: Hearings on H.R. 911 Before the Subcommittee on Improvement of the Legal Profession of the House Committee on Education." According to Rule 15.7, we cite to committee hearings by including the name of the committee, the title, the number of the Congress, the page number, if any, and the full date. If we cite to a particular part of the testimony at the hearings, we include a page number and have the option of including a final parenthetical statement explaining whose testimony we are citing. The title is italicized, and we may abbreviate the name of the committee according to Appendix 3.

H.R. Subcomm. on Improving the Leg. Prof. of the Comm. on Educ., *Excellence in Legal Writing Act: Hearings on H.R. 911*, 104th Cong. 27–28 (Sept. 11, 1999) (statement of Mary Smith).

After hearings, the committee votes to recommend passage of our bill. The committee submits the bill, as amended, in a committee report. Committee reports are good sources of legislative history, including changes to the language of the bill and an explanation of the reasons behind the committee's recommendation. Committee reports are numbered sequentially. A citation to a report, according to Rule 15.9, will include the name of the house, the number of the Congress and the number of the report, a page number, and the exact date of publication. If the House report on our bill is the 83rd report this session, and the report is issued on October 13, 1996, a cite to page 5 of the report would look like this:

H.R. Rpt. 104-83 at 5 (Oct. 13, 1996).

Other types of documents and reports may be issued concerning our bill. Citations to these documents will be exactly as above, except for a different "Rpt." abbreviation. Rule 15.9(a) lists the abbreviations for these various documents.

For some but not all bills, House and Senate reports, as well as recent conference reports, are reprinted, together with the related bill, in the *United States Code Congressional and Administrative News* (abbreviated U.S.C.C.A.N. and informally called "you — scan"). Some reports are also reprinted in the *Congressional Record*. When your legislative resource is available in U.S.C.C.A.N. or the *Congressional Record*, you should include a parenthetical reference to it, as provided in Rule 15.9(g).

H.R. Rpt. 104-83 at 5 (Oct. 13, 1996) (reprinted in 1996 U.S.C.C.A.N. 6144).

H.R. Rpt. 104-83 at 5 (Oct. 13, 1996) (reprinted in 132 Cong. Rec. H4877) (daily ed. Oct. 13, 1996).

Now, back to our bill! Our bill now goes to the floor of the House for a vote. The bill is debated on the floor of the House, and the *Congressional Record* includes a transcript of the debate. The *Congressional Record* is published daily during each legislative session. At the end of each session, all daily editions are published in a permanent, bound edition. The rule governing citation to the debate is Rule 15.12. If the debate is published on page 23,251 of volume 143 of the *Congressional Record*, our citation would look like this:

143 Cong. Rec. 23251 (1996).

If we were citing the debate before the permanent edition of that volume of the *Congressional Record* became available, Rule 15.12 tells us that we would cite to the daily edition. That means that we would give the full date, remembering to abbreviate the month as shown in Appendix 3, and that information would become part of the parenthetical. Notice that an "H" precedes the page number in the daily edition citation because the daily editions are separated into House and Senate proceedings, each with its own consecutive pagination. The page numbers in the separate volumes are preceded by either an "H" or an "S" so you will know which section of the daily edition, House or Senate, to consult:

143 Cong. Rec. H12345 (daily ed. Nov. 15, 1996).[1]

Our bill passes the House! After approval by the House of Representatives, the bill is sent to the Senate for consideration. The Senate will have similar committee hearings and debates on our bill. Once the Senate also passes it, it is assigned a session law number. Most federal session laws are called Public Laws, and Public Law numbers reflect simply the number of the Congress, here the 104th, and the chronological order of the enactment. The law we are tracing is the 205th law enacted by the 104th Congress; therefore, its session law number is Public Law 104–205, abbreviated "Pub. L." as shown in Rule 14.7(a). The session law citation is as follows:

Excellence in Legal Writing Act, Pub. L. No. 104-205 (1997).

Federal session laws are compiled in *United States Statutes at Large*, which, as Rule 14.7(d) indicates, is abbreviated "Stat." Our newly enacted statute appears on page 683 of volume 127 of *United States Statutes at Large*. When the statute appears in that source, its citation will include that information:

Excellence in Legal Writing Act, Pub. L. No. 104–205, 127 Stat. 683 (1997).

When you know where the enacted statute will be codified (usually this information is part of the enacted bill itself), include that information parenthetically in its citation, as Rule 14.7(i) provides. Thus if our statute will be codified as section 1331 of title 53 of the *United States Code*, its citation will reflect this information:

---

[1] On LexisNexis and WESTLAW, all *Congressional Record* cite page numbers are preceded by "H" or "S" even after the document is printed in the permanent edition. However, your citations should follow the ALWD rule of eliminating the "H" or "S" once it is published in the permanent edition.

Excellence in Legal Writing Act, Pub. L. No. 104–205, 127 Stat. 683 **(1999) (to be codified at 53 U.S.C. § 1331).**

Once the act is codified, you will ordinarily cite it as a statute according to the provisions of Chapter 14. However, occasionally you may have a specific reason to cite the bill or the session law. For example, you may wish to cite to the session law when it is codified in many scattered sections or titles of the official code. In addition, you would also want to cite to the original bill to show amendments and to document legislative history. Rule 15.3 tells you to cite enacted bills and joint resolutions just as you would cite unenacted bills and joint resolutions. Rule 15.4 gives you special guidance for citing enacted simple resolutions and concurrent resolutions.

B. Administrative Resources

Just as enacted statutes are positive law, so are the administrative rules and regulations that implement them. Administrative regulations originate with the agencies and departments of the executive branch of government. Take a couple of minutes now to scan the provisions of Rule 19 and familiarize yourself with its contents. Rule 19 covers many types of administrative and executive resources, but we will focus on the most frequently cited sources.

The primary sources of federal administrative materials are the **Code of Federal Regulations** and the **Federal Register**. Rule 19.1 governs final rules and regulations, published in the C.F.R., and Rule 19.3 deals with citing proposed rules and regulations found in the daily editions of the *Federal Register*, as well as administrative notices of numerous kinds.

The C.F.R. is the official compilation of codified rules and regulations and is organized and cited much like the *United States Code*. Both are arranged topically into titles; however, the titles of the U.S.C. and the C.F.R. do not parallel one another. The citation forms are also quite similar. If a rule or regulation has a familiar name, then you may wish to include the name at the beginning of your citation in ordinary type. Just as the title number precedes the abbreviation U.S.C., so the title number of the regulation precedes the abbreviation C.F.R. And just as the section number of the statute follows the code abbreviation, so the regulation section or part number follows its code abbreviation. Also like statutory citations, a citation to a regulation needs a date. This date is the date on the most current volume of the C.F.R., not the date of adoption of the rule or regulation.

statute: *Employee Retirement Income Security Act of 1974*, 29 U.S.C. § 1132 (2000).

regulation: Employee Retirement Income Security Act of 1974, 25 C.F.R. § 2510.3–1 (2007).

or

25 C.F.R. § 2510.3–1 (2007).

Rule 19.1 tells us to cite final rules to the *Code of Federal Regulations* if possible, or to the *Federal Register* if not, indicating parenthetically where the new rule will be codified. (If all this sounds familiar to you, aren't you glad you learned the federal statutory citation material so well?) Each title of the *Code of Federal Regulations* is revised each year, but not all at the same time. The revisions are spread out over four quarterly publication dates, January, April, July, and October. The date of each volume of *Code of Federal Regulations* appears on the cover.

As you have learned (or soon will learn) in legal research, when an administrative agency proposes (or promulgates) a regulation, notice of that proposed regulation is published in the *Federal Register*. When a regulation is adopted in its final form, it will appear first in the *Federal Register* and then in the *Code of Federal Regulations*. The *Federal Register* contains administrative notices, proposed regulations, and other announcements. Rule 19.3 tells us to cite proposed rules, regulations and notices the same way we would cite a final regulation, except that we must include the exact date of the cited *Federal Register* volume.

> Plans Established or Maintained under or pursuant to Collective Bargaining Agreements under Section 3(40)(A) of ERISA, 65 Fed. Reg. 64 (October 27, 2000).

If you cite only a part of a rule, as with a pinpoint citation to any source you must indicate in the full citation not only the beginning page of the rule, but also the specific page on which the cited material appears. The following pinpoint citation to a final rule demonstrates this:

> Grants to Combat Violent Crimes against Women on Campuses, 64 Fed. Reg. 39774, 39777 (July 22, 1999).

Although most of the administrative materials you will have occasion to cite in law school and in your law practice will probably be of the regulatory type, presidential proclamations, Attorney General opinions, and executive orders are also administrative materials, and we cite them according to Rules 19.7, 19.9, and 19.12. Proclamations and executive orders that are currently in force are published in the C.F.R. If a source is not published in the C.F.R. you may cite to the *Federal Register*.

> Exec. Or. 12781, 3 C.F.R. 373 (1992).

Short forms for citations to C.F.R. and the *Federal Register* are discussed in Rule 19.2 and Rule 19.4, which parallel short forms for statutes. For example, if you had already given a full citation for the following final rule:

> 18 C.F.R. § 385 (2007).

then a later citation to the same section after intervening cites would take the following form:

> 18 C.F.R. § 385.

See how easy it all is? Take it away, citation wizards!

Exercise 14

Legislative Resources

A. Legislative History

Put the following information in correct *ALWD* citation form. All sources are being cited in citation sentences in a brief to be filed in a federal court of appeals. Although this exercise builds on the rules used in the previous exercises, this exercise focuses on Rules 15.1, 15.7, 15.9, 15.12, 15.17, 14.2 and 14.6.

1. You want to quote some testimony from a committee hearing. The title on the cover of the published document is "California Desert Lands: Hearings on H.R. 518 and H.R. 880 before the Subcommittee on National Parks, Forests and Public Lands of the House Committee on Natural Resources." The language you are quoting appears on page 96. The hearing took place on June 15, 1993, during the first session of the 103d Congress.

   _____

   _____

   _____

2. In a discussion of the legislative history of the Truth in Lending Act, you cite a session law called the Truth in Lending Class Action Relief Act, published in volume 109 of *United States Statutes at Large* at page 161. The bill was passed in 1995 and given the public law number 104-12.

   _____

   _____

   _____

3. You want to use the definition of the term "federal mandate" that appears on page 6 of a Senate report, number 104-1, published on January 11, 1995. The report was reprinted in the 1995 volume of the *United States Code Congressional and Administrative News* beginning at page 4; the precise language you are quoting appears on page 10 of that publication.

   _____

   _____

   _____

4. In a brief you wish to cite to a statement made by Representative Richard Gephardt on March 24, 1999, during the House debate on H.R. 104-1141, called the FY Emergency Supplemental Appropriation Bill. The statement is published in the permanent edition of volume 145 of the *Congressional Record* of that date. The portion of the debate you are citing appears on page 1617.

_____

_____

_____

B. Administrative Resources

Put the following information in correct *ALWD* citation form. All sources are being cited in citation sentences in a brief to be filed in a federal court of appeals. Although this exercise builds on the rules used in the previous exercises, this exercise focuses on Rule 19.

1. In your brief you are citing a rule concerning prohibitions on political activities applicable to attorneys and staff attorneys of the Legal Services Corporation. The rule is found in title 45 of the *Code of Federal Regulations*, at section 1608.6. The volume of title 45 was published in 2008.

_____

_____

_____

2. You want to cite a regulation of the National Labor Relations Board that appears in the 2008 volume of title 29 of the *Code of Federal Regulations* as section 102.3.

_____

_____

_____

3. You are citing a rule concerning pilot project exemptions to certain rules implementing the National School Lunch Program. It appears in title 7 of the *Code of Federal Regulations* as section 210.19 in part 210. The publication date of title 7 is 2008.

_____

_____

_____

4. You are citing a proposed rule of the Federal Communications Commission proposed on July 1, 2003, and published in volume 64 of the *Federal Register*, beginning at page 35832. The title of the rule is Assessment and Collection of Regulatory Fees for Fiscal Year 2004.

_____

_____

_____

5. You are citing a proposed rule published on May 18, 1999, in the *Federal Register*, volume 64, at page 26844.

_____

_____

_____

6. You are citing to Presidential Proclamation number 7623, made by President George W. Bush on Veterans Day, November 6, 2002. This proclamation appears in volume 67 of the *Federal Register* on page 68751.

_____

_____

_____

7. You wish to cite to Executive Order No. 13268, issued by President George W. Bush on July 2, 2002, terminating the national emergency declared on July 4, 1999 with respect to the Taliban. This order appears in volume 67 of the *Federal Register* on page 44751.

_____

_____

_____

Chapter 15

ELECTRONIC, INTERNET & NONPRINT SOURCES

We have discussed how to cite to most print sources: cases we find in reporters, statutes we find in compilations, legislative history documents found in various government publications, and even common books, magazines and newspapers. However, each year the legal profession moves away from researching dusty volumes in corners of law libraries to "paperless" research. Many (if not most) cases, statutes, legislative history documents, and secondary sources are also available through electronic databases or on the Internet. Not only have commercial electronic databases such as Westlaw and LexisNexis become standard tools of the trade at many, if not most, law firms, but also Internet websites hosted by governmental or commercial entities have become numerous and easy to use. Part 4 of the *ALWD Manual*, Chapters 38 through 42, walks us through the proper citation forms for the various alternative sources for primary and secondary legal materials. In addition, Rule 40 contains citation forms for websites, and Rule 41 even tells us how to cite to electronic mail.

The *ALWD Manual* states its preference that legal writers cite to traditional printed sources for reasons of broad accessibility, authoritativeness, and permanence. However, the *ALWD Manual* does recognize that sometimes sources will be found only in nonprint sources or will be much easier to access using a nonprint source. Because our ultimate goal is to enable our reader to easily access the source using the information in our citation, the authors warn us of the ephemeral nature of some Internet sites. Therefore, legal writers should remember to print out Internet materials and not trust that the source will be there tomorrow. Note that you use the citation format given in Rule 39 for Westlaw and LexisNexis regardless of whether you accessed their databases using a software package and a modem or using their Internet websites.

A. Electronic Databases

Rules 12.12, 14.5, and 39 tell you how to cite material found in electronic databases. Rule 12.12 governs citation of cases found on LexisNexis and Westlaw. If a case is not published in a reporter, then you may cite to one of these commercial databases that does contain the case. You should include the following information:

- the case name,
- the database identifier, which usually includes the year and the database abbreviation (LEXIS, WL), and a unique document number, and
- a parenthetical containing the court abbreviation and exact date of the decision.

Case Name, Database Identifier (Court Month Day, Year).

State v. Werner, 1998 WL 283537 (Wash. App. June 2, 1998).

As with general case citation, if the database identifier is identical to the court abbreviation, then you do not repeat it in the court and date parenthetical.

Bush v. Gore, 2000 U.S. LEXIS 8430 (Dec. 12, 2000).

Notice that Rule 12.13 instructs you to include blanks for reporter information if the case will be printed in the reporter but has not yet been published.

If you wish to use a pinpoint citation to focus your reader's attention on a particular page, remember that the pages given in the reporter are not as useful on a computer screen. Commercial databases assign pages in a process called "star pagination." A pinpoint to one of these pages would contain the word "at" and then an asterisk and the page number, even in the long form of the citation.

Case Name, Database Name/Number **at *Pg** (Court Month Day, Year).

State v. Werner, 1998 WL 283537 at *2 (Wash. App. June 2, 1998).

The unique database identifier is retained in constructing a short form to a case found on an electronic database.

Werner, 1998 WL 283537 at *2.

Rule 14.5 governs citation of statutes found on LexisNexis and Westlaw. When citing a statute available on an electronic database, include the following information:

- the regular statute citation, and
- in the parenthetical, the name of the database and the date through which the statute is current.

Statute Citation (Database current through Month Day, Year).

Tex. Fam. Code Ann. § 8.010 (LEXIS current through 2001 Reg. Sess.).

If Appendix 1 gives publisher information for the unofficial code, include that information as well.

Okla. Stat. Ann. tit. 12, § 2404 (West, Westlaw current through 2002 Reg. Sess.).

Rule 39 seems to apply to all research sources other than cases and statutes found on Westlaw or LexisNexis. However, the examples given are all secondary sources. Accordingly, probably the most convenient feature of electronic databases is the easy searching of secondary sources. When you cite these sources to an electronic database, cite as you would to the printed resource, with an explanatory parenthetical containing the unique database identifier or the name of the provider and the database.

Stephen R. Heifetz, *Blue in the Face: The Bluebook, the Bar Exam, and the Paradox of Our Legal Culture*, 51 Rutgers L. Rev. 695 (1999) (available at 51 RULR 695).

B. Internet Sources

Rule 38.1 expresses a preference for print sources over electronic sources. However, if a source is only available on the Internet or if an Internet citation would facilitate reader access to the source, an electronic citation may be used.

1. Sources Available Only on the Internet

Rule 12.15 governs citations to cases available only on the Internet. Rule 40 governs citation to other sources. When a case is available only on the Internet, Rule 12.15 tells you to include the name of the case and a neutral citation format (covered in Chapter 2, Case Location) or the Uniform Resource Locator (URL), and a parenthetical with the court abbreviation and exact date of decision.

Case Name, URL (Ct. Month Day, Year).

San Antonio Area Found. v. Lang, http://www.supreme. courts.state.tx.us/opinions991117o.htm (Tex. Nov. 9, 2000).

Rule 40.0 focuses on websites on the World Wide Web, not particular sources that are also available on the Web. The citation form for any website will contain:

- author or owner,
- title,
- URL,
- access or update information, if necessary, and
- exact date.

CALI, *Deconstructing the Law School Classroom*, http://www.cali.org/ dlworkshop.html (updated Dec. 15, 2000).

Rule 40.1(a) tells us that the "author" is either the person or organization that wrote the information being cited or, if not available, the host of the site. The title is also a little tricky. Sometimes you wish to refer to the site, so you use the title of the main "homepage." Other times, you may want to cite to a particular page or section. Then, you will include that title after the main title.

Peter Tellers, *Lessons from the Web, There is Something Foul in Legal Education*, http://jurist.law.pitt.edu/lesdec00.htm (Dec. 15, 2000).

When giving the URL, include the entire address from the location you are citing.

If the URL will not take the reader directly to the source cited or if the URL is very long, Rule 40.1(d)(3) allows you to include the protocol (e.g., http://), the domain name (e.g., www.stcl.edu), and the directory in which the file appears. After that information, you may identify keystrokes that will take the reader to the page you are citing. Rule 40.1(d)(3) suggests keystroke identifiers "select," "path," and "search." Use "select" when the reader would have to answer a question of some sort to proceed further. Use "path" when the reader simply needs to follow a path of links (see example below). Use "search" when the reader can only retrieve the document by conducting a search with specific search terms. Separate the URL from the keystroke information with a semi-colon, and separate keystrokes from one another with a comma.

Author, *Title*, URL; *keystroke identifiers* (Access or update information Month Day, Year).

South Texas College of Law, *Practice Exams — Bergin*, http://www.stcl.edu; *path* Faculty/Professor Profiles/Kathleen A. Bergin/Link to Practice Exams.

The date in the parenthetical may simply be the date provided on the site. If you are citing to a document with a separate date, and that document will not be revised or updated, such as an article on a news or magazine website, give the date the article was posted. If the website gives a date as "updated," then include in your parenthetical "last updated." Lastly, if the site does not give any date, give your reader the date you accessed the site.

Community of Christ, *Years of Confusion and Disorganization (1844–1860)*, http://www.cofchrist.org/history/disorganization.asp (accessed May 2, 2005).

2. Sources Available in Print and on the Internet

Rule 38.1 addresses sources that are available in both print and electronic format. In Rule 38.1(a), we see that we should cite to the print source if one is available. However, if the print source is difficult to locate, you might also want to give your reader a URL to find the information online. Rule 38.1(b) and the examples that follow show us how to include an electronic citation with a print citation.

Cite for Print Source (available at URL).

Howard Fineman, The McCain Mutiny, Newsweek 22 (Feb. 14, 2000) (available at http://www.newsweek.com).

Exercise 15

Electronic, Internet & Nonprint Sources

Put the following information in correct *ALWD* citation form. All sources are being cited in citation sentences in a brief to the United States Supreme Court. Although this exercise builds on the rules used in the previous exercises, this exercise focuses on Rules 12.12, 12.15, 14.5, 38, 39, and 40. Although the *ALWD Manual* allows you to introduce certain electronic sources with either "available in" or "available at," the ICW will only be able to recognize one correct answer. Therefore, you should use "available at" for this exercise. You should follow the convention of placing one space after a colon, period, or question mark within a title.

1. State of Connecticut versus Tania Thomas. This is an October 7, 2008, case from the Appellate Court of Connecticut. At this time, the case is not yet published in a reporter. However, it is available on Westlaw. The unique database identifier is 2008 WL 4426789. The docket number for the case is No. 27797. [*Note: A case that has not yet been published is not the same as an opinion that has been designated "unpublished" by the court.*]

2. William McCleery versus Consolidated Edison of New York, Inc. This is a September 16, 2008, case from the New York Court of Appeals. This case is not yet published in a reporter. However, this case is available on the New York Court of Appeals website at http://www. nycourts.gov/courts/appeals/decisions/sep08/ssm23ent08.pdf.

3. "Vetting McCain's Health Plan", an article by Jane Bryant-Quinn, published in the October 13, 2008, issue of Newsweek on page 25. The article is also accessible online at http://www.newsweek.com/ id/162335?tid=related/. Providing an Internet source will substantially improve your reader's access to this article.

4. "Towards a Theory of Assimilating Law Students Into the Culture of the Legal Profession," an article by Marie A. Monahan, published in 2001 in volume 51 of the Catholic University Law Review. The article appears on page 215 of the consecutively-paginated journal. The article is also available on Westlaw in the JLR database.

---

5. House of Representatives Report 107-45, released on April 20, 2001, by the Committee on the Judiciary. The report does not appear in U.S.C.C.A.N. This report is more easily accessible at ftp://ftp.loc.gov/pub/thomas/cp107/hr045.txt.

---

6. You want to cite a statement of Senator Byrd that was made on the floor of the Senate on November 18, 2002. The transcript of this debate is found in the daily edition of the Congressional Record, volume 148, page S11241, where you accessed the remarks. The report is also more easily accessible at http://thomas.loc.gov; path Most Recent Issue, November 19 Senate, Homeland Security.

---

7. You are researching Texas law for an office memorandum. Your law office does not have any state materials, but you have found the applicable provision, Texas Alcoholic Beverage Code § 101.31, using LexisNexis. The screen in LexisNexis states that the text as it appears is current through the 2007 Regular Session.

---

8. In researching the same issue from #7, you find a 1966 related case, Frank Ybarra versus the State of Texas, decided by the Texas Court of Criminal Appeals. The case appears in volume 401, page 608, of *South Western Reporter*, Second Series. Again, your law firm does not have this reporter, but you find it on LexisNexis. The unique identifier given by LexisNexis is 1966 Tex. Crim. App. Lexis 1079.

---

9. In doing some research for a brief, you find a case from the Court of Appeals of North Carolina styled Robert A. Zander, an individual, Plaintiff, Pro Se versus Greater Emmanuel Pentacostal Temple. This case was decided on November 19, 2002. This case is unreported, but you find it online at http://www.aoc.state.nc.us/www/public/coa/opinions/2002/unpub/020174-1.htm.

_____

_____

_____

10. "Copyright Infringement in the Internet Era," an article by Alex Colangelo, published in 2002 in volume 39, page 891, of Alberta Law Review. You found this article on LexisNexis in the Law Reviews Combined file of the Secondary Legal Library.

_____

_____

_____

Chapter 16

WHEN DO I CITE?

We have often found that in teaching our students the intricacies of legal citation rules, we need to stop and focus on the most important citation rule: The rule that tells us when we must cite! Knowing when to cite can be tricky until you have some experience in writing legal memoranda, court documents, or a scholarly paper. You probably have brought some citation placement experience with you from your undergraduate or graduate work. For better or worse, legal writing requires very precise and usually frequent citation of the propositions in our legal writing — probably more precision and frequency than writing in other fields. Rule 43 of the *ALWD Manual* will be a very helpful reference to you for determining when to include a citation.

The general rule of thumb for legal memoranda and court documents is that you need a citation for every fact, thought or opinion that comes from another source (not you or your facts). Rule 43.2 reminds us of this basic tenet. You need a citation even if you are not quoting. The purpose of your citation is to enable your reader to go to a specific page of a specific source and find support for the sentence preceding the citation. If you are detailing the facts of a case or the holding of a case, then you need a citation to that case, whether you are quoting or paraphrasing. If you are quoting or paraphrasing a statute or regulation, then you need a citation. If you are making a proposition about the state of the law generally, then you need a citation to a source that supports that proposition. If you are providing your reader with a rule that you have synthesized from several sources, then you need cites to those sources. Here are some examples of the types of sentences you will write in a legal memorandum or a court document that would need citations:

> In our jurisdiction, courts look to numerous factors when determining whether an individual can establish ownership by adverse possession. *Belotti v. Bickhardt,* 127 N.E. 239 (N.Y. 1920).

> The Court of Appeals of New York held that the defendant's possession must be hostile and under a claim of right; the possession must be actual; the possession must be "open and notorious"; the possession must be exclusive; and the possession must be continuous for a period of twenty years. *Belotti v. Bickhardt,* 127 N.E. 239, 241 (N.Y. 1920).

> The defendant used and rented all portions of a building, a portion of which was built on property owned by the plaintiff. *Belotti v. Bickhardt,* 127 N.E. 239, 240 (N.Y. 1920).

Usually, your entire sentence will be supported by a single citation. In these cases, your citation will immediately follow your textual sentence in a separate *citation sentence.* The examples above are citation sentences. (Notice that they appear as regular sentences and are not in parentheses, unlike other humanities citation systems.) However, Rule 43.1(b) tells us that if only part of our sentence relates to the citation, then we need to insert a *citation clause* immediately following that part of the sentence. If the clause appears between text, then it is set off by commas. If the clause appears at the end of the sentence, it is set off by one comma and ends the sentence with a period.

> Although prior to 1962, the required period for adverse possession was twenty years, *Belotti v. Bickhardt*, 127 N.E. 239 (N.Y. 1920), the current statutory period is ten years, N.Y. Real Prop. Actions & Proc. Laws § 501 (McKinney 1979).

Rule 43.1(c) gives us a third citation device: the embedded citation. With an embedded citation, the full cite of a source is incorporated into the text of your sentence, and you do not add any citation clause or citation sentence.

> In *Belotti v. Bickhardt*, 127 N.E. 239 (N.Y. 1920), the court looked to several factors to determine whether an individual can establish ownership by adverse possession.

Although both the citation clause and the embedded citation are unavoidable at times, some legal readers do not like the interruption of the flow of the text. For this reason, use these citation techniques with discretion. You may choose to rewrite your sentence to utilize the preferred citation sentence.

Note, however, that you do not need a citation when detailing your own facts or even applying a previously cited rule to your facts. If in doubt, ask yourself: "If my reader turns to this page of this source, would the reader find support for this statement?" Here are some examples to illustrate:

> Tina Trespasser, our client, should be able to show that she meets all five of the requirements to prove adverse possession.

> Tina, like the defendant in *Belotti*, has continuously occupied the land in question and earned income from it.

Notice that some of the examples in this chapter cite to the first page of the case only, while others pinpoint the location of specific material cited. When authority is used to represent a rule of law (*e.g.*, a landmark decision like *Roe v. Wade* for the right to privacy), then the citation does not necessarily require a pinpoint. However, when your citation follows facts or reasoning from the case, a pinpoint citation is needed to help your reader find the information cited.

Now that you know how to cite and when to cite, you're all set!

Exercise 16

When Do I Cite?

For this exercise, you will use a set of facts about a fictitious client and two actual cases. You will be given sentences taken in order from a hypothetical discussion section in a legal memorandum. You will need to decide whether each sentence requires a citation to one of the given cases. If you determine that the sentence does not require a citation, then simply leave the space after the sentence blank. (If you are doing this exercise on the website, then type "no citation" in the solution box and click "submit."). If you determine that the sentence does require a citation, then simply type either "Exxon" or "Gonzalez" in plain type as applicable. All citations will be citation sentences.

Facts: Your client is Kendall Loeb. Mr. Loeb lives across the street from a convenience store, The Quik Shop. On August 7, 2001, in the parking lot of the store, Mr. Loeb had an argument with another customer. The customer threatened to kill him and then sped out of the parking lot. Mr. Loeb asked the store attendant, who heard the threat, to call the police, and the attendant refused. As Mr. Loeb was walking back to his house, the customer returned in his truck and hit Mr. Loeb with the truck. Mr. Loeb has filed suit against the store for negligently failing to protect him from the other customer's assault.

Cases: *Exxon Corp. v. Tidwell*, 867 S.W.2d 19 (Tex. 1993). This is the most recent Texas Supreme Court opinion that states the general rule that a landowner has no duty to protect invitees on the premises from criminal acts of third parties. An exception to this rule occurs when the owner both has direct control of the safety and security of the premises and could have foreseen the criminal acts. This case does not focus on the "foreseeability" exception. The rule and exceptions are stated on page 20 of the court's opinion.

Gonzalez v. S. Dallas Club, 951 S.W.2d 72 (Tex. 1992). This case focuses on the "foreseeability" exception. The court specifies the circumstances in which a criminal act would be foreseeable. The court's holding and rationale are on page 76. The facts appear on page 73.

1. Mr. Loeb can prove that the criminal actions of the perpetrator were foreseeable as a matter of Texas law.

   _____

   _____

   _____

2. In Texas, a business owner will be liable for criminal actions of a third party that occur on the premises only if the actions were foreseeable by the owner.

   _____

   _____

   _____

3.   In addition, the business owner must have direct control over the safety
     and security of the premises in order to be liable in a failure to protect
     cause of action.

     _____

     _____

4.   In our case, Mr. Loeb will have to prove that the assault of the customer
     was foreseeable by the store clerk.

     _____

     _____

5.   In Texas, a criminal act of a third party is foreseeable if the owner or his
     agent knew or should have known either that (a) a specific confrontation
     would result in an assault once the parties left the premises or (b) the
     assault was a common type of crime that occurred in that area.

     _____

     _____

6.   Because the area was not a high-crime area, Mr. Loeb will have to prove
     that the store clerk knew or should have known that the confrontation
     between Mr. Loeb and the customer would result in an assault after Mr.
     Loeb left the store.

     _____

     _____

7.   In a Texas Supreme Court case *Gonzalez v. South Dallas Club*, the court
     held that an owner cannot foresee a later criminal act when he takes all
     necessary steps to provide for the safety of a customer exiting the
     premises.

     _____

     _____

8.   In *Gonzales*, the owner escorted a nightclub patron to her car and
     watched her drive safely away.

     _____

     _____

9. Unlike the owner in *Gonzales*, the Quik Shop clerk refused to take any steps to provide for the safety of Mr. Loeb, even when the clerk was told that Mr. Loeb was in danger.

_____

_____

_____

10. Because the resulting assault was foreseeable and because the clerk refused to take any steps to safeguard Mr. Loeb, the court should find the Quik Shop negligent for failing to protect its invitee, Mr. Loeb.

_____

_____

_____

Chapter 17

COURT DOCUMENTS: TRIAL & APPELLATE

So far, we've focused on how to cite authority. However, the law isn't the only material that comes from external sources. The facts also come from external sources. And just as legal readers use the citations in your document to locate and verify the authority you've cited, legal readers also need citations to locate and verify the facts and allegations to which you apply the law in your analysis. Those facts are recorded in a variety of court documents, and those court documents compose what's called the "record" of the case. To fully understand what the record is, you need to first know how documents make their way into the record. Although specific practices vary from jurisdiction to jurisdiction, the general practice of accumulating the record is similar across the country. This chapter will use civil actions in federal courts for illustration.

The first document filed in a case is, of course, the complaint. When a document is "filed," that means it has been submitted to the clerk's office for that court. The clerk's office will start a file for that case and assign it a number. That number is called the "docket number." From that point forward, all documents filed in that case should have that number printed on them, and all documents will be placed in that file in chronological order behind the complaint. Therefore, the next document in the file behind the complaint will likely be some responsive pleading by the defendant. After the initial pleadings in the case, the other documents listed in Rule 29.1(b) may be filed.

A. Citing Documents During the Trial Process

While the case makes its way through the trial process, the parties may want to refer back to documents already filed. For example, a Motion for Summary Judgment might refer back to facts stated in the Complaint. When the facts from the Complaint are referenced, the writer will need to cite the Complaint. To cite documents filed in the same case, you would consult Rule 29. Read through Rule 29 before continuing with this chapter.

1. Full Citation Form

A basic court document citation consists of the abbreviated document name, a pinpoint reference to the material cited, and the exact date of the document.

The first part of a court document citation is the abbreviated name of the document. For guidance in forming abbreviations for court documents, use Appendix 3. Appendix 3 contains abbreviations for words commonly found in court document titles. In addition to abbreviating words, you may eliminate articles and prepositions in the document name when they are not needed for clarity.

| | Defendant's Brief in Support of Motion for Summary Judgment |
| becomes: | Def.'s Br. Supp. Mot. S.J. |

| | Plaintiff's Motion to Compel |
| becomes: | Pl.'s Mot. Compel |

When a person's name is part of the document title, the full name should be included in the citation:

| | Affidavit of Carlton Wells |
| becomes: | Aff. Carlton Wells |

| but NOT: | Aff. Wells |

The second part of the court document citation is the pinpoint reference for the material cited. Rule 29.2(b) tells you to use the most specific reference possible.

cited by page number	Pl.'s Br. Supp. Mot. Quash Subp. 15
cited by paragraph number	Def.'s Ans. ¶ 4
cited by item number	Pl.'s Req. Prod. No. 7

If you have a choice between citing by paragraph number or page number, consider which reference would be most helpful to your reader. If a document is one or two pages long (like an affidavit or short motion), reference the paragraph number to help the reader immediately pinpoint the information cited.

(Mot. Dismiss ¶ 4.)

(Pl.'s Mot. Compel ¶¶ 9-12.)

However, if the document is more than two pages and the paragraphs are not already numbered (as they would be in a federal complaint), reference the page number so your reader can avoid the unnecessary task of counting paragraphs for several pages until she reaches the material cited.

Def.'s Br. Support Mot. S.J. 14

The final element of the document citation is the date parenthetical. Rule 29.2(c) requires the full date, with the month abbreviated according to Appendix 3. The general rule with regard to the date is to provide the most "official" date possible. Therefore, if the document is filed with the court, provide the date of filing. If it is not filed with the court, provide the date the document was served on opposing counsel, which should be the date on the certificate of service.[1] If the document was neither filed nor served, use the date the document was prepared. If none of these dates can be determined, include the abbreviation "n.d." in the date parenthetical.

---

[1] If the date on the certifcate of service is *not* the actual date of service, use the actual date of service for the citation.

With regard to formatting document citations, notice that citations to court documents, unlike citations to authority, may be formatted in bold type, included in parentheses, or both. Although all three are correct under Sidebar 29.1, the ICW will expect the document cites to be enclosed in parentheses with no bold typeface.

(Pl.'s Mot. Directed Verdict ¶ 4 (Mar. 12, 2004).)

Even though the citation is enclosed in parentheses, it is still considered a citation sentence, and the period is placed just inside the closing parenthesis. However, if the record cite is in a citation clause, it will not contain a period.

Dr. Carter admits that his treatment plan was unorthodox (Def.'s Ans. ¶ 12) but denies that it was negligent (*Id.* ¶ 14).

Rule 29.3 provides a specific citation form for trial, hearing, or deposition transcripts.[2] The format is very similar to the form for other court documents. The citation starts with the abbreviated transcript name and ends with the date on which the transcribed proceeding occurred. In the pinpoint reference, though, the citation form makes a few modifications to account for the differences between typed documents and transcribed testimony.

The first difference between typed documents and transcribed testimony is that every line of transcribed testimony is numbered for easy reference to specific statements. The second difference is that transcribed testimony is often so lengthy that it must be divided into multiple volumes. For example, a single deposition may be divided into three volumes of transcribed testimony. Therefore, the pinpoint reference identifies both the page and line number(s) of the testimony cited as well as the volume number if the transcript is divided into multiple volumes.

(Depo. John Carter 75:18 (Dec. 5, 2003).)

(Depo. William Claxton vol. 4, 163:2 (Feb. 2, 2004).)

2. Short Citation Form

Rule 29.4(a) tells you to use "*id.*" if that is appropriate under the circumstances. However, if "*id.*" is not appropriate, Rule 29.4(b) tells you to create the short form of a document citation by omitting any given names or initials from the document name and by omitting the date parenthetical.

---

[2] The appropriate title for a deposition is not clear from the ALWD Manual. The example in Rule 29.3(b)(2) indicates that the title would be "Deposition of X," but the example in Rule 29.4(b) indicates that the title would be "Transcript of the Deposition of X." Although either method of titling a deposition would probably be acceptable, you should choose one method and use it consistently throughout the document. The ICW will expect you to cite it as "Deposition of X."

	(Def.'s Br. Support Mot. S.J. 39 (Oct. 31, 2003).)
becomes:	(Def.'s Br. Support Mot. S.J. 39.)

	(Aff. Jan W. Bryant ¶ 9 (Nov. 3, 2003).)
becomes:	(Aff. Bryant ¶ 9.)

If "id." is the short form you use, it should be formatted like your other citations to the record (*i.e.*, in parentheses, bold, or both).

B. Citing Documents on Appeal

When a case begins the appellate process, documents filed with the trial court clerk's office are referred to as part of the record ("R.") rather than as individual documents (*e.g.*, "Pl.'s Mot. Compel"). The documents in the clerk's file are consecutively numbered, beginning with the complaint and ending with the last document in the case. At that point, all material is referenced by page number rather than paragraph number. A line number may be added to the pinpoint reference for clarity. Therefore, the Complaint might have been cited like this during the course of the trial:

(Pl.'s Compl. ¶ 3 (July 25, 2003).)

However, when the parties refer to the Complaint in the appellate briefs, it would be cited like this:

(R. at 1:14.)[3]

And there you have it! For the record, you're ready for the exercise!

---

[3] Rule 29.5(a) gives you the option of formatting the record cite in a number of ways. The ICW exercise will look for a format consistent with this example: (R. at pg:line.)

Exercise 17

Court Documents

Put the following information in correct *ALWD* citation form. All cases are being cited in citation sentences in a brief to a federal district court. This exercise focuses on Rule 29. You will also need to refer to Appendix 3 for abbreviations of words commonly used in court document titles.

1. In a Motion in Limine, you wish to cite page 3 of the November 5, 2008, affidavit of Meredith Grey, M.D. To date in this litigation, Dr. Grey has only sworn one affidavit.

   _____

   _____

   _____

2. Without any intervening cites, you again want to cite to page 3 of Dr. Grey's November 5, 2008, affidavit.

   _____

   _____

   _____

3. In the same Motion in Limine mentioned in #1 and #2, you wish to cite to paragraph 13 of the Defendant's Second Amended Answer, prepared on July 14, 2008, served on July 15, 2008, and filed on July 15, 2008.

   _____

   _____

   _____

4. In a Motion for Summary Judgment, you wish to cite to paragraph 3 of Plaintiff's Original Complaint, prepared on July 1, 2008, served on July 3, 2008, and filed on July 2, 2008.

   _____

   _____

   _____

5. In a Motion for Protective Order, you wish to cite page 3 of Defendant's Request for Production, prepared on August 3, 2008, and served on August 3, 2008. To date in this litigation, the Defendant has only filed one Request for Production.

   _____

   _____

   _____

6. In an appellate brief, you wish to cite the testimony of Christina Yang, M.D., Ph.D. Her testimony begins in volume 1 of the trial transcript. You wish to cite her testimony beginning on line 2 of page 75 and ending with line 20 of page 75. The testimony was given on September 5, 2009.

_____

_____

_____

7. Two paragraphs later, in the same appellate brief, you wish to cite to Harrison Cole's deposition testimony. Mr. Cole gave his testimony on December 3, 2008.

_____

_____

_____

8. On page 8 of the same appellate brief, you wish to cite to the judge's denial of the Motion for New Trial. In the consecutively numbered record kept by the court clerk, the order denying the Motion for New Trial is on page 537.

_____

_____

_____